The Other Face of the Moon

The Other Face of the Moon

Claude Lévi-Strauss

Foreword by Junzo Kawada

TRANSLATED BY JANE MARIE TODD

THE BELKNAP PRESS OF HARVARD UNIVERSITY PRESS

Cambridge, Massachusetts, and London, England

2013

First published as *L'autre face de la lune: Écrits sur le Japon,*
Copyright © 2011 Éditions du Seuil

Collection *La Librairie du XXIe siècle,* sous la direction de
Maurice Olender

Copyright © 2013 by the President and Fellows of Harvard College

PRINTED IN THE UNITED STATES OF AMERICA

Library of Congress Cataloging-in-Publication Data

Lévi-Strauss, Claude.
  [L'autre face de la lune English]
  The other face of the moon / Claude Lévi-Strauss with a
preface by Junzo Kawada ; translated by Jane Marie Todd.
      p.   cm.
  Includes bibliographical references.
  ISBN 978-0-674-07292-3 (alk. paper)
  1. Ethnology—Japan.   2. Japan—Civilization.
3. Lévi-Strauss, Claude—Interviews.   4. Lévi-Strauss, Claude—
Travel—Japan.   I. Title.
  GN635.J2.L3913   2013
  306.0952—dc23   2012031605

My thanks to Monique Lévi-Strauss,
who followed every stage in the publication
of this volume with equal parts
attention and generosity.
M. O.

Contents

Foreword

Junzo Kawada

BETWEEN 1977 and 1988, Claude Lévi-Strauss made five trips to Japan in the company of his wife, Monique. Just as he was about to leave for the first visit, the great anthropologist mentioned, in the preface to the unabridged Japanese edition of *Tristes Tropiques*, his attachment to Japan:

> No influence contributed so early on to my intellectual and moral training as that of Japanese civilization. By very modest means, no doubt: my father was a painter and, true to the impressionists, he had filled a large cardboard box during his youth with Japanese prints. He gave one to me when I was five or six. I can still see it: a Hiroshige plate, very worn and lacking margins, which depicted women walking under large pines at the seashore.

Overwhelmed by the first aesthetic emotion I had ever experienced, I used it to cover the bottom of a box, which someone helped me hang over my bed. The print stood in for the panorama you were supposed to discover from the terrace of that little house, which, week after week, I set about filling with furniture and miniature figures imported from Japan, the specialty of a store called La Pagode, located on rue des Petits-Champs in Paris. From then on, a print would reward each of my successes at school. That went on for years. Gradually, my father's box emptied to my advantage. But that was not enough to quell the delight that universe inspired in me and which I discovered through Shunshō, Yeishi, Hokusai, Toyokuni, Kunisada, and Kuniyoshi. Up to the age of seventeen or eighteen, all my savings went toward amassing prints, illustrated books, saber blades and hilts unworthy of a museum (since my means permitted me to acquire only humble pieces), but which absorbed me for hours, if only in laboriously deciphering—armed with a list of Japanese characters—the titles, legends, and signatures. I can therefore say that, in my heart and mind, my entire childhood and part of my adolescence unfolded as much in Japan as in France, if not more so.

And yet I never went to Japan. It was not for lack of opportunities; no doubt, it was in large measure for fear of comparing that vast reality with what for me was still "le vert paradis des amours enfantines" (the green paradise of childish loves [Charles Baudelaire, "Moesta et Errabunda"]).

All the same, I am not unaware of the lofty lessons that Japanese civilization holds in store for the West, if it truly wants to hear them: that, to live in the present, one need not hate and destroy the past; and that there is no work of culture worthy of the name that does not make its place for the love and respect for nature. If Japanese civilization succeeds in maintaining the balance between tradition and change, if it preserves the equilibrium between the world and humankind, if it knows how to keep human beings from ruining the world and making it ugly, if, in a word, it remains persuaded, in conformance to the teaching of its sages, that humankind occupies this earth in a provisional manner and that this brief passage does not create any right to cause irremediable damage in a universe that existed before it and will continue to exist after it, then perhaps there will be a slight chance that the somber prospects with which this book opens, in a part of the world at least, are not the only ones that await future generations.

What we find in this volume is a Lévi-Strauss *in love* with Japan. For the first time, his various works written between 1979 and 2001, unpublished or published in scholarly publications, sometimes only in Japan, have been gathered together (see Sources). Emerging from the variety of these texts is a gaze that, if not indulgent, is at least sometimes generous toward the Japanese—that is the sense I have, at least, as an Africanist anthropologist. This was truly Claude Lévi-Strauss's perspective until the end of his life, as attested especially in the preface to the second Japanese edition of *Tristes Tropiques*.

With the agreement of Monique Lévi-Strauss, I proposed to Maurice Olender that a few photographs, scenes from daily life, be added to this book. Some were taken in Japan in 1986, others at the laboratory of social anthropology at the Collège de France or at the author's home on rue des Mar-

ronniers. Finally, a few special moments were pho-
tographed in Lignerolles, in his house in the country. Claude Lévi-Strauss was buried not far from
there, in the village cemetery, on November 3,
2009.

The Other Face of the Moon

1

The Place of Japanese Culture in the World

IT IS A great honor for me to be asked to participate in the work of the International Research
Center for Japanese Studies, officially founded less
than a year ago. I am profoundly touched and
would like to thank the center's director general,
Mr. Umehara Takeshi, and all his collaborators.
But I will also admit that the subject they have
asked me to discuss—"the place of Japanese culture in the world"—appears tremendously difficult
to me. For various reasons, some practical, others
theoretical, I greatly fear I shall disappoint them,
by proving unworthy of the confidence they have
been kind enough to place in me through this invitation.

First, the practical reasons. Whatever interest I
take in Japan and its culture, whatever charm they
hold over me, whatever the importance of the role
I recognize for them in the world, I am the first to

realize that I have only a superficial acquaintance with your country. The total length of my stays in Japan since my first visit in 1977 does not exceed a few months. What is even more serious is that I do not read or speak your language; it is only through French and English translations that I have been able—but in such a fragmentary manner—to consult your literature, from the most ancient to the most contemporary works. Finally, though your art and artisanship fascinate me, my way of grasping them inevitably remains external: I was not born or reared among these masterpieces; and as for the objects of technical and domestic use, I had the opportunity to know their place in culture and to observe how they were handled only at a late date.

CULTURES ARE BY NATURE INCOMMENSURABLE

In addition to these practical reasons, there are theoretical ones, which similarly make me doubt that I can answer the question posed. Indeed, even if I had devoted my whole life to the study of Japanese culture—which, in order to speak about it with some competence, would not have been too much —the anthropologist in me would still doubt that it is possible to situate any culture objectively relative to all the others. For someone who was not born there, who did not grow up there, who was not educated there, a residue containing the most intimate essence of the culture will always remain inaccessible, even for someone who has mastered the language and all the other external means of approaching it. For cultures are by nature incommensurable. All the criteria we could use to characterize one of them come either from it, and are therefore lacking in objectivity, or from a different culture, and are by that very fact invalid. To make a valid judgment about the place of Japanese culture (or of any other culture) in the world, it would have to be possible to escape the magnetic attraction of every culture. Only on that unrealizable condition could we be assured that the judgment is not dependent either on the culture being examined or on the observer's culture, from which the observer cannot consciously or unconsciously detach himself.

Is there any way out of this dilemma? Anthropology, by its very existence, believes there is, since all its work consists of describing and analyzing cultures chosen from among those most different from the observer's, and of interpreting them in a language that, without misconstruing the originality

3

and irreducibility of these cultures, nevertheless allows the reader to approach them. But on what conditions and at what cost? To clarify the limits that the anthropologist runs up against, allow me to illustrate with an example the foregoing considerations, which may have seemed too abstract.

Even though, given my occupation, I am embarrassed to admit it, I feel so profoundly pervaded by the musical forms that came into being and blossomed in the West in the eighteenth and nineteenth centuries that, in general, exotic forms of music hardly affect my sensibility. I take a professional interest in them but am rarely moved. I must make an exception, however, for Japanese music, which I heard at a late date and which immediately captivated me. That phenomenon intrigued me, and I attempted to educate myself by consulting specialists, to understand the reasons for the irresistible charm exerted by your music on an unprepared listener. I thus learned that the Japanese scale, though pentatonic as elsewhere in the Far East, does not resemble any other. It relies on an alternation of minor seconds and major thirds, that is, on intervals formed, respectively, of a semitone and of two whole tones, with a possible alteration of a whole tone on the fifth degree. Through that close-set opposition between large and small intervals, the Japanese scale admirably lends itself to expressing the movements of the heart. The melody, sometimes plaintive, sometimes sweetly melancholic, awakens in even the listener least familiar with Japanese traditions that feeling of the "pathos of things" that constitutes a leitmotif of sorts in the literature of the Heian period, offering him its perfect musical equivalent.

And yet, at the very moment when the Western listener believes he has fathomed the Japanese soul, as revealed by the concordance between two different registers, he is probably guilty of several misinterpretations. First, behind what he perceives as "Japanese music" in general, there are for you marked differences of era, genre, and style. Second and above all, the music I listen to is not very old. It dates at most to the eighteenth century, that is, to well after the literature I believe I have rediscovered in it. The music that Prince Genji played or listened to probably had a different character, close to modes derived from the Chinese scale, even though that scale, more equal-tempered, seems to us incapable of rendering that sense of impermanence, of the precariousness of things, of the inexorable fleetingness of time.

But it may also be that the inevitably fragmented state of knowledge of someone contemplating a culture from the outside, the gross errors in assessment he is liable to make, have their compensation. Condemned to look at things only from afar, incapable of perceiving their details, it may be owing to the anthropologist's inadequacies that he is rendered sensitive to invariant characteristics that have persisted or become more prominent in several realms of the culture, and which are obscured by the very differences that escape him. In that respect, anthropology can be compared to astronomy at its very beginnings. Our ancestors contemplated the night sky without the use of telescopes and with no knowledge of cosmology. Under the names of constellations, they distinguished groups lacking all physical reality, each formed of stars that the eyes perceive as being on the same plane, even though they are located at fantastically different distances from earth. The error can be explained by the distance between the observer and the objects of observation. It is thanks to that error, however, that regularities in the apparent movement of the celestial bodies were identified early on. For millennia, human beings used them—and continue to use them—to predict the return of the seasons, to measure the passage of time at night, and to serve as guides on the oceans. Let us refrain from asking more from anthropology; however, in the absence of ever knowing a culture from the inside, a privilege reserved for natives, anthropology can at least propose an overall view—one reduced to a few schematic outlines, but which those indigenous to the culture would be incapable of attaining because they are located too close to it.

THE GREAT THEMES OF UNIVERSAL MYTHOLOGY

Along with music, I began my talk with a confession. Allow me to add another, which I hope will make you better understand the way that, as an individual and an anthropologist, I apprehend Japanese culture.

In 1985 I visited Israel and the holy sites, and then, about a year later, in 1986, the places where the founding events of your most ancient mythology are supposed to have unfolded, on the island of Kyushu. My culture, my background, ought to have made me more sensitive to the first sites than to the second. Exactly the reverse occurred. Mount Kirishima, where Ninigi-no-mikoto descended from heaven, and the Amanoiwato-jinja opposite the cave where Ohirume, the goddess Amaterasu, was confined elicited in me emotions more profound than the supposed location of the Temple of David, the Cave of the Nativity, the Holy Sepulchre, or Lazarus's tomb.

Why is that? It seems to me it is because of the very different way that you and we envision our respective traditions. Perhaps because your written history began at a relatively late date, you quite naturally locate its roots in your myths. The transition comes about smoothly, especially since the state in which these myths came to you attests to a conscious intention on the part of the compilers to make them a prelude to history proper. The West certainly has its myths as well, but for centuries it has taken pains to distinguish what belongs to myths from what belongs to history: only attested events are judged worthy of consideration. The paradoxical consequence is that, if the events recorded by tradition are to be taken for real, they must also be locatable. In the case of the holy sites, however, what guarantee do we have that the things happened in the places we are told they did? How could we be sure that Empress Helena, mother of Constantine, who went to Palestine in the fourth century to identify the holy sites, was not a victim of her credulity? And that, a few centuries later, the Crusaders were not similarly deceived? Despite the progress of archaeology, everything, or nearly everything, continues to rest on their assertions. The visitor in possession of an objective turn of mind, even if he does not dispute the veracity of scriptures, wonders not necessarily about the events reported but about the places he is shown as being those where they unfolded.

That is not at all the case in Kyushu, where everything is suffused in an overtly mythical atmosphere. The question of historicity does not arise or, more exactly, it is not pertinent in the context. Without causing any uneasiness, two sites can even compete for the honor of having welcomed the god Ninigi-no-mikoto upon his descent from heaven. In Palestine, places that possess no intrinsic quality must be enriched by myth, but only insofar as the myth claims not to be one—these are places where something *really* happened. But nothing guarantees it was actually *there*. Conversely, in Kyushu, sites of an unparalleled splendor enrich the myths, add an aesthetic dimension to them, make them at once present and concrete.

For Westerners, a gulf separates history from

myth. One of the most absorbing charms of Japan, by contrast, lies in the intimate familiarity one feels there with both history and myth. Even today, one has only to count the buses disgorging visitors to these sacred sites to be convinced that the great founding myths, the grandiose landscapes where the tradition situates them, maintain a real-life continuity between legendary times and contemporary sensibilities.

That continuity could not have failed to strike the first Europeans who visited Japan. Back in the seventeenth century, Engelbert Kaempfer divided Japanese history into three periods: fabulous, uncertain, and true. He thus included myth within that history. And it is to that capacity, perceived early on, for embracing and unifying categories that seem irreconcilable to us that we can attribute the consideration that Western travelers and thinkers had for Japan, even before they came to know it well. In a note to *Discourse on the Origin and Foundations of Inequality among Men*, published in 1755, Jean-Jacques Rousseau enumerates the different cultures about which the West knows nothing or too little, and which urgently need to be studied on site. For the Northern Hemisphere, he cites some fifteen nations and completes his review with these words: "and especially Japan." Why "especially"?

One answer would come a century later. We have forgotten the profound impression that the collections of your most ancient traditions—the *Kojiki* and the *Nihon Shoki*—made on the European scientific world. E. B. Tylor, the founding father of British anthropology, made public their main lines in 1876; and, in the 1880s and 1890s, the first English and German translations appeared.* Some did not hesitate to see them as the most faithful reflection that has come down to us of the great primordial myth—*Urmythus,* the Germans said—which, they thought, must have been common to humanity as a whole at the origin of time.

It is true that, in different styles—more literary in one case, more scholarly in the other—the *Kojiki* and the *Nihon Shoki* link together, with incomparable art, all the great themes of universal mythology, and that this mythology imperceptibly dissolves into a history. Thus arises the fundamental problem of Japanese culture: How are we to ex-

---

* E. B. Tylor, "Remarks on Japanese Mythology," paper delivered on March 28, 1876, *Journal of the Royal Anthropological Institute* 7 (1877): 55–58.

plain how this culture, placed at the far end of a vast continent, occupying a marginal position there, and having experienced long periods of isolation, could at the same time offer in its most ancient texts a perfectly elaborated synthesis of elements found elsewhere in dispersed order?

The problem is not limited to the Old World: these old texts contain many mythological themes and motifs that are also present in the Americas. But on that point, caution is necessary: all these themes common to the Precolonial Americas and to ancient Japan are found in Indonesia, and several are well-attested only in those three regions. We can rule out from the start the hypothesis of an independent invention, given the extent to which the myths of these three regions correspond even in their details. Must we therefore endeavor, as in the past, to discover a single origin for them? According to that hypothesis, either Indonesian or Japanese myths journeyed independently in both directions; or, having departed from Indonesia, the myths first reached Japan and then went on to the Americas. Recent prehistoric discoveries in Miyagi Prefecture have brought to light stone tools forty or fifty thousand years old, vestiges of a human settlement that, by virtue of its northern position, may have been a passageway between the Old and New Worlds.

Let us not forget that, at several times during the great glacial periods and until even recently— about twelve to eighteen thousand years ago— Japan was joined to the Asian continent, forming a long headland curving northward. During the same periods, "Insulindia" (that is, the group of islands located between Taiwan and Australia on one hand, New Guinea and the Malay Peninsula on the other) was also connected in great part to terra firma. And finally, a land bridge about a thousand kilometers wide connected Asia and America at the current location of the Bering Strait. Along the edge of the continent, a boulevard of sorts allowed humans, objects, and ideas to circulate freely from Indonesia to Alaska, via the coasts of China, Korea, Manchuria, and northern Siberia. At different moments of prehistory, that vast entity must have been the site of population movements in both directions. It is therefore better to give up seeking points of origin. In all likelihood, the myths constitute a common patrimony, fragments of which can be collected all over.

THE MOTIF OF THE LOST OBJECT

What, then, does Japanese originality consist of? I shall be able to define it more clearly by examining an episode in your mythology. In 1986 I had the opportunity to contemplate, on the eastern shore of Kyushu, the cave where, as myth would have it, the child U-gaya-fuki-aezu-no-mikoto was raised by his maternal aunt, whom he later married and who became the mother of Emperor Jimmu.

These incidents took place in a context well-attested in Indonesia and the Americas as well. But the remarkable thing is that the Japanese version is the richest, in two ways. It alone contains the entire sequence: first, a pair of brothers endowed with complementary functions; second, the motif of the lost object whose owner demands its return; third, the visit to a king or god of the seas, who not only finds and returns the lost fishhook but gives his daughter in marriage to the brother at fault; and finally, the prohibition, violated by the husband, on looking at his wife when she is giving birth (since she changes into a dragon at that time) and the wife's definitive departure. That last part has its analogue in Europe: according to a fourteenth-century narrative, the fairy Melusina, married to a human, vanished when her husband discovered that she was half-woman, half-serpent—but not before giving birth to a son, a descendant of whom later aspired to marry his maternal great-aunt. In the Japanese version, the son of the princess of the seas marries his maternal aunt. And it is curious, to say the least, that in a South American myth, a story of a stolen fishhook is followed by a case of incest with an aunt—though granted, a paternal aunt. In any event, only certain elements of the Japanese sequence are found in Indonesia, Europe, and North and South America, and not exactly the same ones in each place.

The richer Japanese sequence also has a more rigorous construction. In the *Kojiki** and the *Nihongi*,† the mythic narrative first evokes a major opposition between life and death and then neutralizes that opposition by introducing a third term: the henceforth abridged duration of human life. Within the category of living things, another opposition then arises, this time between two brothers. On the temporal axis, one is older, the other younger; on the spatial but also the functional axis, one

---

* *Kojiki*, book 1, chaps. 41–46.

† *Nihongi*, book 2, chaps. 24–50.

devotes himself to hunting, the other to fishing—
that is, to activities associated, respectively, with the
mountains and the sea. At the instigation of the
younger brother, the two attempt to neutralize the
functional opposition by exchanging their equipment: fishhook for bow and arrows. The brothers
fail, but from that failure itself a temporary success
results: so long as the union between one brother
and the sea princess lasts, the spatial opposition
between land and sea will appear to be overcome.
But just as no one human being can succeed in
combining within his person the gifts of hunter
and fisherman, so too a mediator cannot with im-
punity betray her dual nature: that of human and
that of sea monster. The price to be paid for the
mediation is too high, the husband and wife separate, and the spatial opposition becomes irrevoca-
ble. The *Nihongi* say so explicitly, concluding the
episode of separation with these words: "That is the
reason there is no longer any communication between land and the world of the sea."* Does not
Japan's insular nature make it consubstantial in
some sense with that opposition between land and

---

* Ibid., book 2, chap. 48.

sea and with the endless efforts imposed on human beings to overcome it?

Let us complete the analysis. At the beginning of the sequence, the abridged duration of human life provides a resolution to the antinomy between life and death, which belongs to the temporal dimension. At the end of the sequence, the antinomy between land and sea, which belongs to the spatial dimension, also finds an intermediate resolution: the hero returns from his visit to the king of the seas as the master of tides. The phenomenon of tides gives the advantage sometimes to land over sea, sometimes to sea over land, but in accordance with a periodic rhythm that once more belongs to the temporal order. The birth of Emperor Jimmu, which resulted from the resolution of these cosmic oppositions, completes the circle: at least in the minds of the compilers, myth is left behind with the advent of history.

What are we to conclude from this example, to which several others drawn from your ancient mythology could be added? None of the incidents I have summarized belong properly to Japan. They are found, as I said, in various parts of the world. The motif of the rejected exchange is attested even in Africa (which we know had repeated contact with Asia). But nowhere else were these dispersed elements so forcefully organized, nowhere else did they provide the material for so vast a synthesis, as in your eighth-century texts. Whether they represent vanished models or innovations, they illustrate specific characteristics of Japanese culture. These can be considered from two angles. Given the diversity of the elements that, in very ancient times, must have competed to form a relatively homogeneous ethnic type, language, and culture, Japan was initially a place for people to meet and mingle. But its geographical location at the eastern end of the Eurasian continent, its intermittent isolation, allowed it to function as a filter or, if you like, as an alembic, which distilled a rarer and more subtle essence than the substances transported by the historical currents that mingled there. I find that alternation between borrowings and syntheses, syncretism and originality, the best way to define Japan's place and role in the world.

Prehistory can attest to that phase of meeting and mingling, beginning from the most ancient times. Over the years, it has gradually become clear that the Japanese Paleolithic displays an extraordinary richness: Where else in the world has anyone found—as was the case recently near the city of Akashi—a small wooden board, carved by human hands and dating to perhaps fifty to sixty-five thousand years ago? The variety of stone tools is no less surprising. There is no doubt that, over millennia, different cultures, corresponding to successive settlements or to on-site evolutions, sowed the seeds of diversity in Japan.

The "Jōmon Spirit" and Action Painting

Conversely, a civilization of sedentary hunter-gatherers and fishermen, who did not practice agriculture but who became expert in the art of pottery, presents us with an absolutely original case. The range of human cultures offers nothing comparable to it. Indeed, Jōmon pottery resembles no other: first, by virtue of its age, since there is no ceramic art that dates back to a more ancient time; second, by its longevity, which is on the order of ten millennia; finally and above all, by its style, which achieves its most striking expression in the Middle Jōmon pieces that could be called "flamboyant," but for which there is no basis of comparison, except the most incongruous. Indeed, their often asymmetrical composition, exuberant forms, and modeled decoration, where serrations, cockscombs, excrescences, volutes, and other vegetal sinuosities intermingle, might bring to mind some Art Nouveau of five or six thousand years ago; and, in other respects, the lyrical abstraction or action painting of certain contemporary artists. Even accomplished pieces have a certain sketchiness about them. You might think that the artist was swept up in a sudden inspiration and that each of his works received its definitive form in a spontaneous burst of creativity.

That is a false impression, no doubt, attributable to our ignorance of the use to which these vases were put, and of the social, psychological, and economic conditions specific to a society about which we know almost nothing. In any event, I have often wondered whether, despite the upheavals introduced by Yayoi culture, something of what could be called the "Jōmon spirit" does not persist in contemporary Japan. Perhaps we should attribute to it an invariant trait of the Japanese aesthetic, the speed and sureness of execution, which require on one hand an unsurpassed mastery of technique, and on the other, a long period of meditation before the work to be completed. These two conditions were likely present as well among those inspired virtuosi, the Jōmon potters. And might we not perceive that bizarrely designed basketwork, made of thin strips of bamboo, unequal in size and in rigidity and capriciously intertwined, as a distant and distorted echo of the same stylistic principle? You do not seem to make a large place for such basketry in your exhibitions and museums, but I see it as one of the most curious and, in many respects, one of the strangest expressions of Japanese taste.

Fewer doubts arise about other constants. There are recurrent stylistic traits in the figural representations that appear on the sides of *dōtaku* from the Yayoi period; in *haniwa* a few centuries later; in Yamato art at an even later date; and, very close to our own time, in *ukiyo-e* art. In all cases, an expressive intention and a sobriety of means prevail. For the graphic arts, there is also an opposition, which is also a complementarity, between flat color and line drawing. Nothing is further from profuse Chinese complexity, which at other times or in other domains is an obvious source of inspiration.

Japanese culture thus possesses an astonishing capacity to oscillate between extremes. Like your weavers, who readily combine geometric and naturalistic motifs, pleasure is even taken in juxtaposing contraries. Japan differs in that respect from Western culture, which has also taken different approaches over the course of its history, but which likes to persuade itself that it is replacing one with another, never thinking of turning back. In Japan, the dimensions of myth and history are not felt to be mutually exclusive, any more than originality and borrowing, or, to conclude with the aesthetic aspects, the most advanced refinements of your lacquer and porcelain workers and the taste for rough materials, for rustic works—in a word, for everything Yanagi Sōetsu called the "art of the imperfect." It is even more striking that an innovative country, in the vanguard of scientific and technical progress, has preserved its reverence for an animist mode of thought, which, as Umehara Takeshi rightly pointed out, has its roots in an archaic past. That is less surprising when we observe that Shinto beliefs and rites themselves proceed from a vision of the world that rejects all exclusivity. In recognizing a spiritual essence for all beings of the universe, Shinto unites nature and supernature, the world of human beings and that of animals and plants, and even inert and living matter.

On the Unpredictability of Beings

In the West, lifestyles and modes of production appear in succession. In Japan, they may be said to coexist. But are they in themselves radically different from our own? When I read your classical authors, I feel not so much disoriented in space as out of sync. The *Genji Monogatari* prefigures a literary genre that would become current in France only seven centuries later, with the novels of Jean-Jacques Rousseau: a slow, tangled plot rife with nuance, and evolving characters whose deep-seated motivations escape us, as often happens in real life. Full of subtle psychological commentary, it is awash in a melancholic lyricism that makes as large a place for the feeling for nature as for the sense of the impermanence of things and the unpredictability of beings.

Your great historical chronicles, the *Hōgen Monogatari*, the *Heiji*, and the *Heike* encapsulate a different time lag. Indeed, these works of a grandiose pathos belong to what, in our modern idiom, we would call "feature journalism" and, at the same time, to epic poetry. At the end of a number of chapters, windows open for great flights of lyricism: for example, in the second book of the *Heike*, the tableau of the decadence of Buddhism, the moldering manuscripts, the deteriorating monuments; or, at the end of book 7, the abandonment of Fukuhara by the Heike. I do not find any equivalent to them until our nineteenth-century literature, with Chateaubriand's *Memoirs from beyond the Grave*.

Finally, when I read dramatic works for the Bunraku theater by Chikamatsu, Izumo, Shōraku, Senryū, or Namboku, and the adaptations that the Kabuki made of them, I am overcome by the richness and ingenuity of the plot, by the combination of melodrama and poetry, by the depiction of heroic feelings alongside portraits of the life of the common people. Almost the only thing approaching them in our theater is, in my view, Edmond Rostand's *Cyrano de Bergerac*, which was not performed until 1897. One of your young authors, Shionoya Kei, entitled a book on the relationship between Japanese and French theater *Cyrano and the Samurai*; it recently received an award from the Académie Française.* He could not have chosen a better title.

---

* Shionoya Kei, *Cyrano et les Samuraï* (Paris: Publications orientalistes de France, 1986).

That is not all. Just as the lucidity of Japanese culture allowed it to logically articulate mythical themes that it did not invent on its own (they have even been seen as a sort of paradigm of universal mythology), so too your ancient literature can be called upon to shed light on sociological problems of general import. In a book that appeared two years ago in Japanese translation under the title *Haruka-naru Shisen,** I attempted to show that a romance such as *Genji Monogatari*, and treatises or historical chronicles such as *Eiga Monogatari* and *Ōkagami*, cast such a penetrating gaze on the institutions of the era, analyze so subtly the actors' motives, that the great classic problems that have arisen for sociologists and ethnologists can often be viewed in a completely new light. I am thinking of the marriage of what in our jargon are called "cross cousins" and of the role of maternal kinship in ostensibly patrilineal societies. The Japanese material provides valuable aid in elucidating questions relating to the social organization of scattered peoples from Africa to the American Northwest, questions that for years have confounded ethnologists.

---

* Claude Lévi-Strauss, *Le regard éloigné* (Paris: Plon, 1983).

A Cartesianism of Feelings

If we now ask why, in areas as different as mythology and sociology, Japanese texts ten or twelve centuries old can serve as our models, the answer may be found in certain characteristics of the Japanese spirit, and in the first place, an extreme attention to enumerating and distinguishing all aspects of reality, without leaving any out, granting to each one an equal importance. This can be seen in your traditional manufactured objects, where the artisan treats with the same care the inside and the outside, the right side and the wrong side, the visible parts and those that are invisible. That is still the case, in fact, for products whose nature has been altered by scientific and technological progress. I consider that one of the reasons for the success of your microelectronics: your pocket calculators, tape recorders, and watches are, in a different register, still objects of fine workmanship, as appealing to the touch and to the eyes as your *tsuba*, your *netsuke*, and your *inrō* used to be.

I find evidence of that analytical spirit, that predisposition both moral and intellectual, which for lack of a better term I shall call your "divisionism" (a term usually reserved for a mode of painting that proceeds by juxtaposition of pure colors), in the most diverse sectors of Japanese culture. In your cuisine, of course, which leaves natural products in their pure state and, unlike Chinese and French cuisine, does not mix substances or flavors; but also in the art of Yamato-e, which separates line drawing and flat zones of color; and also in your music. I have already said a little about that, but I would like to return to it so as to underscore this aspect.

Unlike Western music, Japanese music does not possess a harmonic system: it declines to mix sounds. But it compensates for that lack by modulating sounds that have been left in their pure state. Various shifts affect the high notes, the tempos, the timbres. These shifts subtly integrate sounds and noises; for we must not forget that, in the Japanese tradition, the calls of insects, which the West considers noises, belong to the category of sounds. The equivalent of a harmonic system is thus realized over time, by means of tones of various qualities, emitted one after another but within a time span short enough to form a totality. In Western music, several notes sound at the same instant and produce a simultaneous harmony. Yours is successive: it exists nonetheless.

It would probably be going too far to see that

Japanese taste for discrimination as an equivalent of sorts to the rules Descartes formulated and which underlie his method: "Divide each difficulty into as many fragments as required to best resolve it," and "make enumerations complete enough to ensure that nothing is omitted." Rather than a conceptual Cartesianism, I would credit Japan with an aesthetic Cartesianism or a Cartesianism of feelings. Even expressed in that form, the analogy may appear forced, but it helps us understand the appeal Japan has exerted on Western minds since the eighteenth century, as attested by the preponderant place Rousseau recognized for it among all the cultures of the boreal hemisphere.

Sounds, Colors, Odors, Flavors, Textures

Perhaps we could attach a significance that would not be merely symbolic to the respective positions of our two countries, France at the western end of the Eurasian continent, Japan at the eastern end. Separated by vast spaces, located on their fringes — one at the edge of the Atlantic Ocean, the other at the edge of the Pacific — France and Japan appear to be turning their backs on each other. Nevertheless, they share the same fate, since they can be seen as the far reaches where, in opposite directions, influences that had their common origin in Asia came to rest.

On that matter, I would like to quote a thinker and great writer, one whose ideas were distorted and put to the worst use. In 1859 Gobineau said of Asia: "Nothing of what has been found in the world has been found elsewhere. It was then improved, modified, amplified, or diminished; that second-order honor falls to us . . . But it is inventiveness that contains life."* Gobineau was speaking as a Westerner, but it is clear that the philosophical thought of Japan, its religious ideas, and its art were likewise fertilized by currents from Persia and India. Since very ancient times, dating back to prehistory, the Old World was the theater for the intermingling of populations and movements of ideas, which resulted in greater unity than the differences that later arose might lead us to believe. Until historical times, the far eastern and far western border regions of Eurasia, where our two countries are situated, were never totally isolated from each other, as attested by a shared fount of myths and legends.

------

* J. A. de Gobineau, *Trois ans en Asie*, part 2, chap. 7.

The ancient Greeks located the kingdom of Midas, who grew donkey ears, in Phrygia—hence in Asia. The story is repeated in Tibet, Mongolia, Korea, and even Japan, where the *Ōkagami*, an eleventh- or twelfth-century text, clearly alludes to it. In 1983, during a visit to Iheya-jima in the Ryukyu Archipelago, I heard a ritual chant that was translated for me as it was being sung. To my great amazement, I recognized it as a story already related by Herodotus, who places it in Lydia. Conversely, the Buddha became a figure of Christian patrology in the Middle Ages under the name of Josaphat, an approximate but very recognizable transcription of the word *bodhisattva*.

Ōbayashi Taryō, an eminent Japanese scholar, and Professor Yoshida Atsuhiko believe they have rediscovered themes of Indo-European origin in Korea and Japan, in particular the ideology of the three functions elaborated by the late Georges Dumézil. This ideology was supposedly introduced in about the fourth century C.E. by an equestrian people originally from southern Russia. When I had the honor of welcoming Dumézil into the Académie Française, I noted in my speech, regarding these hypotheses, that a tripartite structure similar to that of the Indo-European peoples also existed in western Polynesia. In a comment on that remark, Dumézil was kind enough to confide to me that Marcel Mauss, the master thinker of French ethnology, sometimes wondered aloud whether the Polynesian word *areoi*, which designates a sacred brotherhood, was not derived from the Sanskrit *ārya*, which gave us the term "Aryan." The problem of the existence of the three functions in the Pacific world might not arise only for Japan.

We must be cautious with regard to conjectural history, but many indications suggest that ties were established between the East and the West in prehistoric times. If Europe, that headland of the Asian continent, and Asia proper, including its easternmost regions, were in active communication in the past, we would better understand how Japan, the extreme tip of Asia to the east, and France, the extreme tip of Europe to the west, could illustrate symmetrical states of a series of transformations. "Asia had inventiveness," wrote Gobineau, in the text whose beginning I have already quoted. "By contrast, it lacked criticism as we possess and practice it." And to what country would Gobineau's next comment apply better than to France? "Criticism is our dominant aptitude, it produces the shape of our minds, it is the source of all our pride."

Whereas, in the tradition of Montaigne and Descartes, France may have pursued further than any other people its gift for analysis and systematic criticism in the order of ideas, Japan for its part developed, more than any other people, a penchant for analysis and a critical spirit exerted in every register of feeling and sensibility. It distinguished, juxtaposed, and matched sounds, colors, smells, flavors, consistencies, and textures to such an extent that an entire arsenal of expressive words (*gitaigo*) exists in language to represent them. Whether in your cuisine, your literature, or your art, a supreme economy of means requires that every element be given the task of conveying several meanings. Except for a few peculiarities of vocabulary, Japanese is not a tonal language; but Japanese civilization as a whole appears to be a tonal civilization, where every experience awakens resonances in different registers.

At opposite ends of the Old World, then, two parallel forms of the critical spirit manifested themselves. They acted in antithetical domains, and yet they became counterparts of each other. I see that

as the reason—in any case, as one of the reasons—
that, as soon as the French spirit learned something
about the Japanese, it felt in harmony with their
spirit. From the eighteenth century on, artisans in
France were inspired by Japanese objects, even in-
corporating them as such into their works. Generally impervious to exoticism, Balzac speaks somewhere of the "wonders of Japanese art," not failing
to contrast them, significantly, to the "grotesque
inventions of China."* The contemporaries of Ingres, one of our greatest painters, imputed the distinctive characteristics of his art—the primacy of
line over color, the lack of importance granted to
modeling—to the influence of Far Eastern painting. Let us not forget, finally, that Japonism, which
inspired the impressionists and European art more
generally in the second half of the nineteenth century, had its birth in France. And, at the very beginning of the twentieth century, the discovery, also
French, of the primitive arts might not have come
about if French art lovers and artists had not already acquired from Japan the taste for matters left
in their crude state: rough textures, irregular or
asymmetrical forms, bold simplifications. The raku

---

* In *La recherche de l'absolu* (1834).

ceramicists and the Rimpa school had themselves sought models for such forms in the works of rustic Korean potters. In that sense, the discovery of "primitivism" can be said to be attributable to the Japanese.

By virtue of its demographic density and the number and diversity of its civilizations, the Old World appears to be a full world. But what about on the other side? To the east, Japan looks toward the Pacific Ocean: an empty world, at least at these latitudes. From opposite sides, America and Japan face each other. Solely from the geographical standpoint, the respective positions of France and Japan, and those of Japan and America, are also in a symmetrical relationship. But it is an inverted symmetry, and that inversion manifests itself in several ways.

The discovery of America is rightly seen as a major event in human history. We are beginning to understand that, four centuries later, the opening of Japan was another, though with diametrically opposed characteristics. North America, poor in people, was a new world abounding in unexploited natural resources. When Japan made its entrance on the international scene, it appeared as a new world as well, but poor in natural resources. By contrast, its population constituted its entire wealth, not only in terms of numbers but because of the image it offered of a humanity that was not yet worn down, used up by battles of ideas, revolutions, wars, one that was guided by an intact faith in its values.

Considered from that angle, the Shingaku movement, founded by Ishida Baigan in the eighteenth century, reflected a living reality that sought only to find expression: that of a humanity at the ready, where every individual, whatever his rank and condition, perceived himself as a center of worth, meaning, and initiative. I do not know whether that privilege will last for long, but in Japan nothing is more striking than the eagerness everyone shows to perform his duties well, that cheerful goodwill that, compared to the social and moral climate of the foreign visitor's home country, seems to him to be a key virtue of the Japanese people.

Major Differences between Eastern and Western Thought

By way of conclusion, I should like to show how that dual relation of symmetry, which I believe I have discerned between Japan and Europe (and especially France) on one hand, and between Japan and America on the other, also relates to the responses that Japan has given to problems that arise in both the East and the West.

Western philosophers see two major differences between Eastern thought and their own. In their view, Eastern thought is characterized by a dual refusal: a refusal of the subject and a refusal of discourse. In various modalities, in fact, Hinduism, Taoism, and Buddhism deny what in the West is self-evident at a fundamental level: the self, whose illusory character these doctrines are intent on demonstrating. For such doctrines, every being is only a provisional arrangement of biological and psychological phenomena, with no lasting element such as a "self": it is vain appearance, destined ineluctably to dissolve.

In terms of discourse, the West has believed since the Greeks that human beings have the ability to apprehend the world by using language in the service of reason: a well-constructed discourse coincides with reality, it gains access to and reflects the order of things. Conversely, according to the Eastern conception, all discourse irremediably falls short of reality. The nature of the world in the last instance—supposing that notion has any meaning—escapes us. It surpasses our faculties of reflection and expression. We cannot know anything about it and therefore cannot say anything about it.

Japan reacts in a totally original manner to these two refusals. It does not of course attribute to the subject an importance comparable to that granted it in the West. It does not make the subject the obligatory starting point for all philosophical reflection, for any project of reconstructing the world through thought. It has even been said that Descartes's dictum "I think, therefore I am" is rigorously untranslatable into Japanese.

But it seems to me that Japanese thought does not annihilate the subject either: rather, the Japanese make the subject a result rather than a cause. The Western philosophy of the subject is centrifugal: everything starts with it. The way Japanese thought conceives the subject appears rather to be centripetal. Just as Japanese syntax constructs sentences through successive determinations moving from the general to the specific, Japanese thought places the subject at the end of the line: it is the result of the way that increasingly small social and professional groups fit together. The subject thus recovers a reality; it is, so to speak, the last place where the groups it belongs to are reflected.

That way of constructing the subject from the outside also lies within the Japanese language, which is inclined to avoid the personal pronoun. It lies as well within the social structure, where "self-consciousness" (*jigaishi* in Japanese, I believe) is expressed in and through the sense everyone has—even the most humble person—that he is participating in a collective project. Even tools of Chinese design, like the crosscut saw and various kinds of planes, were adapted in Japan six or seven centuries ago to be used backwards: the artisan pulls the tool toward himself rather than pushing it away. In situating himself at the point of arrival, not at the starting point, of an action performed on matter, the Japanese artisan reveals the same deep-seated tendency to define himself from the outside, as a function of the place he occupies in a determinate family, professional group, geographical environment, and, more generally, in the country and society. It is as if Japan turned the refusal of the subject inside out, in order to extract a positive effect from that negation: to find in it a dynamic principle for social organization that protects it from the metaphysical renunciation of the Eastern religions, from the static sociology of Confucianism, and from the atomism to which the primacy of the self makes Western societies vulnerable.

The Japanese response to the second refusal is of a different order. Japan brought about a complete reversal in a system of thought: placed by the West in the presence of a different system, it retained what suited it and set aside the rest. Indeed, far from repudiating en bloc the *logos* as the Greeks understood it—that is, the correspondence between rational truth and the world—Japan placed itself resolutely on the side of scientific knowledge, which occupies a prominent place in that country. But having paid a high price for the ideological vertigo that took hold of it in the first half of the twentieth century, Japan has become true to itself once more. It abhors the perversions of the *logos* to which systematicity fitfully leads Western societies, and which has ravaged so many Third World countries.

One of your major contemporary thinkers, Professor Maruyama Masao, pointed out the traditional aversion of the Japanese character to phraseologies, its distrust of a priori reasoning, its

attachment to intuition, experience, and practice.*
It is significant in that respect that the abstract notions that the West delights in and which it writes
with a capital letter—Truth, Liberty, Right, Justice,
and so on—are so difficult to express in Japanese.
Significant as well is the fact that the neutralist
theory of evolution, attributable to Kimuro Motoo,
appeared in Japan and nowhere else. No theory
could be more useful in aiding Western thought to
liberate itself from its tenacious prejudices: that all
natural phenomena are marked by rationality and
that a logical necessity guides them in a direction
similar to the one that we ourselves assign to our
own actions.

Vis-à-vis the East and the West, therefore, Japanese culture occupies a unique place. In a distant
past, Japan received a great deal from Asia. It received a great deal from Europe in a more recent
past, and even more recently, from the United
States. But all these borrowings were so carefully
filtered, their finer substance so well assimilated
that, up to now, Japanese culture has not lost its
specificity. Nevertheless, Asia, Europe, and Amer-

---

* Maruyama Masao, *The Intellectual Tradition in Japan*
(*Nihon no Shisō*) (Tokyo: Iwanami Shoeten, 1961), p. 75.

ica can find in Japan images of themselves profoundly transformed. Today in fact, Japanese culture offers the East the model of social health and the West that of a mental hygiene, whose lessons it behooves those countries, borrowers in their turn, to take to heart.

2

The Hidden Face of the Moon

MR. PRESIDENT, Ladies and Gentlemen, let me assure you that I am infinitely touched by the great honor that the organizers of this colloquium have done me by inviting me to speak at its closing session. At the same time, I cannot fail to be aware of the overwhelming irony of the situation in which I find myself. For truly, if you had wished to end with a kind of practical experiment, in which you would demonstrate the urgency, the importance, the necessity of developing Japanese Studies in France, you could certainly not have done better — like a psychiatrist who introduces a patient to his audience — than to bring in someone like me, who knows absolutely nothing about the subject. Or perhaps you had a different notion: that, after the sessions, some with the austere dignity of Noh theater, others turbulent like a Kabuki play, you might present toward the end a little Kyōgen play of sorts, in which the role of the innocent would fall to me. Lost among the learned scholars, the poor fellow would show by his blunders that he cannot distinguish a fan from an umbrella—as in *Suehirogari*—or, through the reflections he presents to you, that he is all too prone to take bladders for lanterns, as we say in French. But in the end, I am ready to assume that role, if only out of gratitude toward the Japan Foundation, which allowed me, during a visit that I hardly dare admit did not surpass six weeks, to reach a real turning point in my thinking and my life.

That trip, exactly two years ago, coincided with the adoption of a work proposal—one among others—by my laboratory, devoted, precisely, to the notion of work. We were struck by the observation that, in the populations ethnologists study, there is not always a word for "work"; and when the word does exist, its meaning does not necessarily coincide with its use in French. Where we have one word, another culture might have several. It is therefore important to seek in different cultures how manual and intellectual work, agricultural and artisanal work, sedentary and itinerant work, men's and women's work are conceived and even named—because of course one must begin with linguistics. It is also important to seek what sort of relationships the worker of whatever kind maintains with his tools. I remember a conversation on that subject with Professor Yoshida Mitsukuni, in his pretty house in Kyoto on the slopes of Mount Hiei. He pointed out the personal attachment that the Japanese artisan sometimes has to his tools. Finally, it is imperative to discover what relationship to nature such work presupposes. Is it an entirely active relationship on one side, that of the human being, and passive on the other, the side of nature, as the West generally conceives it? Or does that relationship assume the character of a true cooperation between humans and nature, as in other civilizations? At a Noh performance, during which he constantly sought to enlighten me, Professor Watanabe Moriaki, who is in attendance today, remarked to me that work has a true poetic value in Noh, precisely because work represents one of the forms of communication between humans and nature.

I therefore asked the Japan Foundation to organize my trip wholly as a function of questions of that sort, that is, to put me in contact with artisans, with workers, and preferably not in the big cities but in somewhat remote corners of the country. I shall therefore not speak to you of the museums, the temples, the sanctuaries, the landscapes I visited, or even of the Kadomi storehouses in Kuroshima, which were one of the highlights of that trip. Rather, I shall speak of my encounters, from Tokyo to Osaka and from Kyoto to the Oki Islands in the Sea of Japan, in Kanazawa, Wajima, Takayama, Okayama, and other places, with pastry chefs and sake brewers, potters and sabersmiths, weavers, dyers, kimono painters, gold beaters, wood turners, lacquer decorators using every technique (from *chinkin* to *makie*), carpenters, fishermen, traditional musicians, and even cooks.

ILLUSORY EXOTICISM

I shall not go into detail. What I will tell you is the provisional conclusion, whether true or false, that I drew from these encounters. Not surprisingly — and once again, I plead the excuse of being a neophyte — I had the impression that the profound difference between Japanese and Western artisanship, and the relative success that the Japanese forms have had in persisting, unlike their Western counterparts, lie a great deal less in the survival of ancient techniques, which all in all have survived in

Western Europe as well (except, perhaps, the truly prodigious knowledge of the uses of all parts of the plant: flowers, leaves, sap, roots); that the difference, I say, may not lie so much in the better or greater survival of techniques—after all, there are marvelous techniques that persist in the Faubourg Saint-Antoine in Paris and elsewhere—as in the relative preservation of family structures. Upon my return, inasmuch as I was able to communicate my Japanese experiences to government officials in France (who, as you know, are concerned with protecting artisanship), my advice was oriented toward preserving family structures, establishing particular benefits, or building larger facilities for artisanal businesses that still have that type of structure, so that they could survive and develop.

At the same time, I realized on further reflection that, contrary to what I had initially believed, what I had gone to seek in Japan was the image, probably illusory, of an exoticism that is, so to speak, less spatial than temporal. That is, I wanted to find what I would call zones where traces of preindustrial society might survive, better preserved perhaps in one sector or another than is the case in Europe. These zones would have such specific characteristics that, in an attempt to understand them, I would immediately be impelled to undertake all sorts of readings about Japan's past, going back as far as I could in time. In that respect, I would be following the example of the Japanese themselves, for whom —I was struck by this fact—the Heian period is a sort of absolute frame of reference.

I quickly ran into problems, which presented themselves to me as paradoxes. I had previously read the *Genji Monogatari* in the Waley translation: I reread it in the Seidensticker translation and also read part of the translation that René Sieffert is beginning to publish. Every step of the way, I was flabbergasted by what I found. These are, of course, astonishing sources for the ethnologist, with all sorts of infinitely detailed indications on the role of maternal kinship and on the psychology of marriage between cross cousins. This was a moment, precisely, when a society in the process of historical change was affirming its will to become historical and wanted to distance itself from such marriages, because liberation from the rules of marriage, the possibility of choice, was also the possibility of speculation, of adventure, of treaties and contracts. At the same time, what did that long, slow, tangled romance with little action but rife with nuance bring to mind? What did it echo in our own literature? What I am about to say may be a truism, I don't know, it may have been said a thousand times before me: I repeat, I am speaking as an ignoramus and a neophyte. I could find only one point of reference, one term of comparison, and that is Jean-Jacques Rousseau's *New Heloise*. Furthermore, in both the *Genji* and in Rousseau, at a distance of several centuries, I recognized a relationship between the author and his characters that in the West would come to the fore only much later on, for example, in Dostoevsky and Joseph Conrad. It is the idea of a psychological fantastic, an opacity of human motives, which can only be grasped through external manifestations and results. The psychological operations that are actually unfolding in the minds of the characters are never comprehensible. Simultaneously, that opacity gives us the sense that we are in the presence of truth itself, that these are things that can happen, that do happen in reality.

With your permission, let me quickly compare the two plots. *The New Heloise:* a woman, who marries a man much older than she, confesses to him that she formerly had a lover; and the husband has nothing better to do than to summon that lover and oblige him to live near her, leading them both to unhappiness. We shall never know whether the husband, in acting in that way, was impelled by sadism, masochism, a hazy moral philosophy, or quite simply by foolishness. And when I consider the chapters in the *Genji* called, I believe, the "Uji chapters," what is the story about? Two boys get worked up over two women they have never seen and are thereby led to ruin. It seems to me that this is the same psychological climate, providing the same level of access, so to speak, to human psychology.

I then became absorbed in the *Hōgen*, the *Heiji*, and the *Heike Monogatari*, courtesy of Sieffert's translations, and once more, I was met by surprise after surprise. For here again, the ethnologist finds astonishing material in that civilization of adolescent headhunters where life ends at twenty, plus indications not only about the dualist organization that ethnologists study in much more rudimentary societies but also about the development of that organization. If I am not mistaken, in fact, in Heian-ky there were initially geographical halves, east and west, which in the Kamakura period shifted around to become north and south, and were transformed from purely geographical divisions into hierarchical halves.

During my trip to Japan, I identified traces of that type of organization in other cities and other regions. Wajima was formerly divided—and not all that long ago—into two halves, the "masters of the city" and the "residents," who were inferior to them. In Nakakoshima in the Oki Islands, the two ancient villages, north and south respectively, practiced endogamy among the common people, who married only within their own village, and exogamy among the upper classes, through an exchange of wives between villages. But in addition to being ethnological documents, those old works have a "feature journalism" side: they are "slices of life" of a grandiose pathos. Think of the account of the murder of Tameyohsi's children. And there again, I wondered what echo there might be of that in our literature. That rare combination of a chronicler, a memorialist, who is at the same time a feature journalist and who, at the end of the chapters, opens wide the windows to flights of lyricism of a poignant melancholy (for example, in the second book of the *Heike*, the tableau of the decadence of Buddhism, with moldering manuscripts, moss-covered monuments, temples in ruin; or, at the end of the seventh book, the abandonment of Fukuhara by the Heike), I do not find that in our literature until the Chateaubriand of *Memoirs from beyond the Grave*.

What, then, is this Japan, which from our perspective short-circuits genres, telescopes periods, and which, between the eleventh and the thirteenth century, delivered to us all at once, and all in a jumble as it were, archaic facts and literary genres marked with a refinement, a subtlety, a sensibility that would appear in Europe only six or seven centuries later? It is not at all surprising that this problem arises for us; and it is even less astonishing that it arose for me personally when I perceived it for the first time. What surprised me is my impression that it arises for the Japanese themselves. Throughout the duration of my trip I, who knew nothing about the matter, was constantly confronted with a question: "What do you think of us, what do you believe we are, are we really a people, we who in our past combined Euro-Siberian elements, others from the South Seas, who were influenced by Persia via India, then by China and Korea, who were then subjected to the influence of the West, whereas now the West is slipping away altogether, and we no longer even have a solid base of support in it?" Hence that latent question and the bizarre impression that, like others before me to be sure, I was in Japan not only to be shown it and to look at it but also to provide the Japanese with an opportunity, never fully realized, to look at themselves in the image I formed of them. What could I reply to my Japanese colleagues and friends, based only on the elements available to me? Not a great deal, of course. I could only tell them, in my ignorant naïveté, that there can be no doubt about the identity and originality of a country whose music, graphic arts, and cuisine display characteristics unlike any other.

GRAPHIC ARTS AND CUISINE

I will speak very little of music, because I would not be competent to explain the reasons for the sense of absolute originality one feels when listening to Japanese music, by which I mean traditional music. What I find striking, however, is that each of the instruments it uses is distinguished by its geographical origin and that the system of notation varies for each instrument, also as a function of geographical origin.

As for the graphic arts, allow me to make a slight digression on a subject that was rather thorny throughout my stay, because it irritated my Japa-

nese friends. By that I mean the print, an art that
was a revelation to me when I was six or so, and
about which I have never since stopped being pas-
sionate. How many times have I been told that I
was interested in vulgar things that were not true
Japanese art, true Japanese painting, but were on
the same level as the cartoons I could cut out from
Le Figaro or *L'Express!* That irritation eased somewhat at times, especially in Kyoto, where, in a
rather seedy Shimonsen shop, I found a triptych—
oh, not very old, from the Ansei period—whose
existence I was aware of and which interested me
because of certain American parallels. Done by
one of Hiroshige's students, it depicts the battle
between the fish and the vegetables, a very old
theme (*irui gassen*) dating to the Muromachi period and attributed to a prime minister and poet,
called, I believe, Ichij Kanera. That theme persisted through the ages and was still alive in the
mid-nineteenth century, in the vulgar form of *gete-
mono*. And then again, at the Historiographical Institute at the University of Tokyo, I asked to consult
the collection of popular images—an object of
great disdain, I must say—relating to the Edo earthquake of 1855. There I found documents that, it
seems, Cornelis Ouwehand did not have before

him and which could considerably enrich our view of the mythology of earthquakes in the nineteenth century.

The French might be even more annoyed, fearing we might fall into truisms about the Goncourts and the impressionists. I would like instead to take a view that goes completely counter to commonplace notions, since it seems to me that the great interest of the print as it developed in the eighteenth and nineteenth centuries was that it showed something very profound about Japanese art—I apologize for speaking about this next to Mr. Akiyama, who will be able to correct my blunders. That something appears, it seems to me, with its definitive characteristics at the end of the Heian period, in the illustrations of the "Lotus Sutra." It persists via the Tosa school, and bursts forth in the three admirable portraits attributed to Fujiwara Takanobu that André Malraux found so striking. That something is not at all Chinese and can be defined as the independence or dualism of the expressive line and flat color. The print, better than any other technique, was able to manifest that independence, since the wood engraving is by nature ill-suited to render the brushstroke, which, by contrast, seems to me characteristic of Chinese painting. Paradoxically, in Europe that independence, that autonomy of line and color, elicited the enthusiasm of the impressionists, who in their art did exactly the opposite. If they had truly understood it, the Japanese print would not have led to Monet, Pissarro, or Sisley but would rather have brought about a return to Ingres, in whom we find exactly that same dualism, which in fact shocked his contemporaries.

Finally, let me say a word about cuisine, with apologies for being so down-to-earth. But you know that the study of food has played a certain role in my books, since nothing is more important in my eyes than the way that human beings undertake to incorporate the natural world into themselves. Shall I make a confession besides? I fell instantly in love with Japanese cuisine, to the point of introducing into my daily diet two years ago both seaweed and rice cooked by the rules. Well, having tried all sorts of cuisines in Japan, from *sansei* to *kaiseki*, and having had very long and fruitful conversations with cooks, here again it seems to me that there is something totally original, and that nothing is further removed from Chinese cuisine than that cuisine with almost no fat, which presents natural products in their pure state and leaves the combination of them to the choice and subjectivity of the consumer.

With both the graphic arts and cuisine, then, I believe I can see at least two invariant traits. In the first place, there is a moral and mental hygiene directed toward simplicity: an isolationism, a separatism, since both a graphic art in the purely Japanese tradition and a purely Japanese cuisine do not mix different things together but rather highlight their basic elements. I have heard—I don't know if it's true—that one of the differences between Chinese Buddhism and Japanese Buddhism is that in China, different schools coexist in the same temple, while in Japan there have been since the ninth century exclusively Tendai temples and other, exclusively Shingon temples—another manifestation of that effort to keep separate what ought to be so. But at the same time, an extraordinary economy of means sets the Japanese spirit apart from what Motoori Norinaga, an author who has been quoted a great deal in the course of this colloquium, called, I believe, "Chinese pompous verbosity." That extraordinary economy of means dictates that each element acquire a plurality of meanings; in cuisine, for example, a single product will have a seasonal connotation, an aesthetic presentation, and a particular consistency distinct from its flavor.

The Calls of Insects

Japanese may not be a tonal language, or is just barely one; but I would readily say that Japanese civilization appeared to me to be a tonal civilization, where each thing belongs simultaneously to several registers. And I wonder whether that resonance, that evocative capacity of things, is not one of the aspects connoted by the enigmatic expression *mono no aware*. The spareness goes along with the richness: things mean more. I have learned from reports that a Japanese neurologist, Dr. Tsunoda Tadanobu, has demonstrated in a recent work that his compatriots, unlike all other peoples, even those in Asia, process the calls of insects in the left hemisphere of the brain rather than the right hemisphere, which suggests that for them the calls of insects are not noises but are rather on the order of articulated language. And in fact, can you imagine the hero of a Western novel undertaking, like Genji, to have insects transported to his garden from distant moorlands, so as to delight in their song?

Despite these differences, Europe in the eighteenth and then the nineteenth century was able to recognize essential values in Japanese art, values incomparable to their own. I have also pointed out that the most ancient Japanese literature puts us face to face with our own points of reference, but arranged differently. Japan for its part has proven capable of equaling and even, in certain areas, of surpassing the West. Beyond the differences, therefore, a certain complicity, relations of symmetry, and reflections must exist between us.

In the Japanese language, it appears, the speaking subject usually expresses his intention to leave his home while qualifying it with the indication that he will return shortly. During my stay, I was struck by the fact that the Japanese artisan saws and planes in the opposite direction from our own: toward himself, from the object to the subject. Finally, it was in reading Maruyama Masoa's excellent book *Studies in the Intellectual History of Tokugawa Japan* that I truly understood that Japan sought to equal the West at the start of the Meiji period, not in order to identify with the West but rather to find the means to better defend itself against it. In these three cases, as a result, a centripetal movement stands opposed to a centrifugal movement as we conceive it in the West. That is, in realms as varied as spoken language, technical activity, and political thought, there is the same astonishing ability to pull oneself together.

As I continued to muse, I was led to compare what happened in Japan in the Meiji period to what had happened in France a century earlier, in 1789. Indeed, Meiji marked the transformation, the shift from feudalism (I do not use the word in the rigorous sense; I heard in this very forum pertinent observations on that subject) to capitalism, whereas the French Revolution prompted the simultaneous destruction of expiring feudalism and of nascent capitalism by a bourgeoisie of bureaucrats and a peasantry hungry for property. But if the revolution in France had also come about from above, from the king, instead of occurring against him—stripping the nobility of its privileges inherited from feudalism but leaving it its wealth—perhaps that would have allowed the rise of big business, into which only the nobility had begun to venture. Eighteenth-century France and nineteenth-century Japan were faced with the same problem: how to integrate the common people into the national community. If 1789 had unfolded in a manner comparable to the Meiji Restoration, perhaps France would have become the Japan of Europe in the late eighteenth century.

Allow me to add one final consideration, not simply as a French colleague but as an Americanist. For the last few years, it has appeared probable that several Indian languages of California (Wintun, Maidu, perhaps even all those belonging to what is called the Penutian family) are in reality Ob-Ugric languages: languages of the Uralic family from western Siberia.

I will not venture speculations about the coherence or fragility of the Ural-Altaic family; but if languages of the Uralic family truly exist on the Pacific Coast of North America, as we may now believe, it is clear that an Altaic language existing in that same Pacific would have had a much greater range than has previously been assumed. Japan would then appear to be a sort of outlier, an accumulation of successive strata that have been described and named but that rest on a foundation that could almost be called Euro-American, and to whose existence Japan alone would attest.

In that case, for anyone approaching history not,

so to speak, from the visible face of the moon—the history of the Old World beginning with Egypt, Greece, and Rome—but from its hidden face, which is that of the Japanologist and the American-ist, the importance of Japan's history would become as strategic as that other history, that of the ancient world and of Europe in archaic times. We would then have to imagine that the most ancient Japan could have played the role of a bridge of sorts be-tween Europe and the Pacific as a whole. It and Europe would have been responsible for develop-ing—each on its own side—symmetrical histories, both similar and opposing, somewhat in the way that the seasons are reversed on either side of the equator, but in a different register and on a differ-ent axis. It is therefore not only from the Franco-Japanese standpoint, which was that of this collo-quium, but within a much vaster perspective, that Japan may seem to hold certain of the master keys providing access to what remains the most mysteri-ous sector of humankind's past.

3

The White Hare of Inaba

THERE HAS BEEN general agreement for a long time that the story of the hare of Inaba is a minor animal tale. It is represented in southeast Asia in many versions, which Klaus Antoni has inventoried.* But I intend to look in an entirely different direction today. As it happens, the myths of North and South America include similar narratives and give them an importance that sheds light on the story of the hare of Inaba.

It is the South American versions that are closest to that story. A hero (sometimes it is a heroine), pursued by an enemy, pleads with a caiman (the South American crocodile) to take him across a

_____

* *Kojiki*, trans., intro., and notes by Donald L. Philippi (Tokyo: University of Tokyo Press, 1968), chap. 21; Klaus J. Antoni, *Der weisse Hase von Inaba: Vom Mythos zum Märchen* (Wiesbaden: Franz Steiner, 1982).

river. The saurian agrees, but not without ulterior motives. He demands that his passenger insult him (a good pretext for devouring him); or he accuses him of having insulted him; or he is in fact insulted by the hero who, after arriving safe and sound, believes he will be able to escape.* This is the closest to the two known Japanese versions, in which the hare, having barely set foot on the bank, makes fun of the crocodile and reveals that the crocodile has been deceived.

THE THUNDERBIRD

The episode takes on much greater scope in North America. It appears in a great myth of the Mandan Indians, who settled on the upper Missouri River and lived from cultivating corn and hunting buffalo. They had a very complicated ceremonial life. The myth accounts for the calendar of rites that marked the important moments of the year.

The myth tells of two brothers who, having pursued various adventures, reached the home of an agricultural deity, the mother of corn. They spent a

---

* See Claude Lévi-Strauss, *Le cru et le cuit* (Paris: Plon, 1964), p. 259.

year with her, then sought to return to their village. A river cut off their route. They crossed the river on the back of a horned serpent, which they had to feed to keep up his strength; otherwise, the serpent claimed, they all ran the risk of going under. But when the brothers, upon reaching the other side, leapt onto the bank, the serpent swallowed one of them. The other, advised by a nearby thunderbird, managed to free his brother by offering the serpent fake food. The thunderbird led the two brothers to his heavenly dwelling, where they performed all sorts of remarkable feats. After a year, the thunderbirds took them back to their village and ordered that ceremonies in their honor be celebrated every autumn.

I cannot reproduce in detail the long analysis of that myth, to which several pages of *The Origin of Table Manners* are devoted.* I shall limit myself to highlighting two points. Note first that the myth comprises three sequences. The first concerns an earthly stay with an agricultural deity, the third a heavenly stay with a war deity. As for the second

---

* Claude Lévi-Strauss, *L'origine des manières de table* (Paris: Plon, 1968), pp. 359–389.

sequence, it concerns a journey, not a stay, and unfolds on the water.

The second point has to do with the heroes' conduct. When they are with the agricultural deity, the two brothers must behave with moderation: they are permitted to hunt, but discreetly and in limited quantities. By contrast, at the home of the thunderbird, their conduct is marked by immoderation: without heeding the advice to be cautious, they attack monsters and kill them. Since water is an intermediate element between sky and land, the conduct of the two heroes toward the water serpent is itself intermediate between moderation and immoderation: it consists of haggling, dupery, false promises. That ambiguous behavior, which in the American myth appears as a logically necessary consequence and which could have been deduced from the other two, is the same as the conduct of the hare of Inaba toward the crocodile. One might consider it a gratuitous detail in that case, but in America it is integrated into a totality, where it finds its meaning.

In the *Kojiki*, the story of the hare of Inaba constitutes the inaugural episode of what could be called the "epic of the great god Opokuninusi," which takes up chapters 21 to 37.* Recall that the following episode has to do with the god's love rivalry with his brothers, who, to wreak their revenge, subject him to supposedly deadly ordeals. One of these ordeals especially will hold our attention: the brothers chop down a tree, split the trunk in two with an ax, and separate the two halves by inserting a wedge. Then they force their younger brother into the gap and remove the wedge, so that the trunk closes up again, crushing the victim.

Now that motif, without example elsewhere, is typical of American myths about an uncle or father-in-law who seeks to do in his nephew or son-in-law. Indexed as H1532 in Stith Thompson's *Motif-Index* and as 129 in his *Tales of the North American Indians*, it was given the code name "wedge test" by American mythographers. It is noteworthy that the thirty or so versions inventoried are concentrated in the United States and Canada, in a region west of the Alaska Range and the Rocky Mountains. Franz Boas, considering a myth present in Oceania and Japan and concentrated in the same region of

---

* The transcription of the names of the gods and the divisions into chapters of the *Kojiki* are those of D. L. Philippi (1968).

the Americas, concluded more than a century ago
that its origin lay in the Far East. It is difficult to
escape the same conclusion regarding the wedge
test.*

The conflict between Opokuninusi and his elder
brothers, during which he is reduced to servitude
but nevertheless wins the favors of the princess
whom they had claimed for themselves, belongs to
universal mythology, despite a few alterations. As
good methodologists, we should therefore not grant
a particular meaning to it. Let us note, however,
that the *Kojiki* associates it with the episode of the
touchy ferryman or conveyor, with whom one must
haggle or whose services must be obtained through
deception. And the American versions of the myths
about a jealous relative or relatives also make that
association. Furthermore, they combine into a sin-

---

* There is a weak version of the uncle or father-in-law motif,
however, in the story of Milo of Croton. See Stith Thompson, *Motif-Index of Folk-Literature*, 6 vols. (Bloomington:
Indiana University Press [printed in Copenhagen by Rosen-
kilde & Bagger], 1958); also *Tales of the North American Indians* (Cambridge, Mass.: Harvard University Press, 1929),
pp. 269–386. See also Franz Boas, *Indianische Sagen von der
Nord-Pacifischen Küste Amerikas* (Berlin: A. Asher, 1891–
1895), p. 352.

gle narrative certain motifs that in Japan are the
object of distinct and merely adjoining narratives.
For example, a hero, falsely accused by his sister-in-
law (his elder brother's wife), is abandoned on a
desert island in the middle of a lake; he will persuade a sea monster to take him across the lake
and return him to land.* In short, the connection,
which appears arbitrary in the *Kojiki* (the protagonists are not the same), and for that reason has
given rise to much speculation, is motivated in the
American myths.

Let us now come to the following episode in the
Opokuninusi epic, which unfolds at the home of
the god Susanowo. It has its exact equivalent in
America, in what are called the "evil father-in-law"
myths. The most common versions recount that a
young hero, often socially disgraced or of miracu-
lous birth, ascends to heaven to marry the daughter
of the Sun. Susanowo is not a sun god, of course,
but the place he chooses to stay (*Kojiki*, chap. 13.6),
and where Opokuninusi goes as well (chap. 23.1),
undoubtedly has characteristics of a "world beyond." In any event, in Japan as in America, the

---

* See, on this subject, Claude Lévi-Strauss, *L'homme nu*
(Paris: Plon, 1971), pp. 401, 462–463.

hero, having reached his destination, meets the daughter of the master of the house. She falls in love with him and takes him to her father, who agrees to the marriage but seeks to do in his son-in-law by subjecting him to ordeals, which, he believes, the young man will not survive. In Japan and America, the hero survives thanks to the magical assistance of the young woman, who takes her husband's side against her father.

The Crane and the Crocodile

Before I can show that America, unlike Japan, also makes a motivated place in this mythical series for the ferryman episode, I must digress for a moment.

The North American myths represent the touchy ferryman either as a crocodile (an alligator in that part of the world) or as a crane. The crocodile is mobile: he moves from one bank to the other. As for the crane, she stands on the opposite shore, from which someone calls to her, and merely stretches out one of her legs to be used as a footbridge. She requires praise or gifts from those asking for safe passage. If she approves of them, she warns that her knee is fragile and must not be damaged; in the contrary case, she is silent, her supposedly damaged knee gives way, and the passenger falls into the water.

Like the crocodile, which reveals by his unwillingness and his demands that he is only a half-hearted ferryman, a "semiconductor," so to speak, the crane allows only a portion of those who appeal to her to get across. She transports one category of clients in complete safety but intercepts the others and drowns them.

A digression within the digression: I learned from a recent article by Edwina Palmer that, according to several *Fudoki*, a guardian deity located in the mountains would give safe passage only to one traveler in two, or fifty out of a hundred, or simply half, and would kill the rest.* Might there exist in Japan, as in America, mythical beings with a "semiconductor" function? I confine myself to pointing out the problem and now return to the motif of the evil father-in-law, which the American myths combine with that of the ferryman.

A myth of the Salish-language Indians, who live on the Pacific Coast in what is now the state of

* Edwina Palmer, "Calming the Killing *Kami*: The Supernatural Nature and Culture in *Fudoki*." *Nichibunken Japan Review* 13 (2001): 3–31.

Washington, portrays two brothers, or sometimes several, the youngest of whom commits a great deal of foolishness. Pursued by an ogre that he had unwisely invited to dinner, the brother arrives at the edge of a river and hails a crane he perceives on the other side. That crane is Thunder, with whom the hero must bitterly haggle for assistance. Thunder finally consents to take the brother across the river, offers him hospitality and the crane's daughter in marriage. At this point, Thunder imposes ordeals — foremost among them the wedge test — that ought to kill the hero, but which he overcomes thanks to his wife.

Hence the ferryman and the evil father-in-law, who in the *Kojiki* are separated by a distance of two chapters and are distinct characters, sometimes constitute a single character in American myths.

It is therefore clear how the myth of Opokuni-nusi and the American myths we have compared to it are both similar and different. In both cases, we find the coalescence of the same motifs or themes: touchy ferryman, jealous relative or relatives, evil father-in-law, ordeal of the split tree trunk (and perhaps a counselor mouse, which would require a more thorough study). But the Japanese myth juxtaposes these motifs or themes, whereas the American myths organize them. Like a skeleton in an ancient tomb whose bones no longer fit together but remain so close that it is possible to see they once formed a body, the proximity of the elements in the myth of Opokuninusi suggests that, as in the American myths, they were once organically linked.

What are we to conclude from that? It is as if a mythological system, perhaps native to continental Asia and whose traces would have to be discovered, had gone first to Japan, then to America. The system is still identifiable in Japanese mythology through disconnected remnants that remain contiguous in the narrative. In America, perhaps because of the later arrival of the myth, their unity would be more perceptible. According to that hypothesis, the presence in the *Kojiki* of the story of the hare of Inaba would not be fortuitous. Although it seems unrelated to the episodes that precede and follow it, it would bear witness in its way that it was an integral part of a mythological system, of which the American examples give us some idea. Specialists in Japanese mythology—more competent than I, but prompted by the hypothesis I submit to them—will perhaps manage to connect the threads.

4

Herodotus in the China Sea

In May 1983, after a stay in Tokyo, I was given the opportunity to accompany two Japanese colleagues who were pursuing their research in Okinawa and in the neighboring islands of Iheya, Izena, and Kudaka.

Since I have no knowledge of the language or a fortiori of the local dialect, I will not claim that my observations add anything whatever to the many studies on Ryukyu culture that have been conducted for nearly a century by Japanese, American, and European scholars (including a Frenchman, Patrick Beillevaire, who is in attendance today). I took part in my colleagues' investigation as a spectator, from time to time venturing a question, which they were kind enough to translate for me, along with the informant's response.

The pages that follow have no other ambition, therefore, than to serve as a backdrop to an incident—the only one, of all those I noted down, that may have some originality—which it does not seem out of place to include in a miscellany in honor of a Hellenist.

MASCULINE TO THE EAST, FEMININE TO THE WEST

The incredible population density of the coastal zones leaves anyone visiting Japan for the first time dumbstruck. That is not at all the case in the Ryukyu Islands: with its subtropical vegetation, limited in height by typhoons and reduced near the sea to a very dense thicket of pandanus, no human presence can be detected for one or sometimes two kilometers.

Even there, however, evidence abounds, largely imperceptible to the untrained eye, of a highly original culture, one that, amazingly, is recognizable as that described by the first observers in their time.

A main street, running north to south, still divides each village into halves. These moieties continue to supply the two teams that face off every year in a tug-of-war (two ropes are used, each folded back on itself and hitched one inside the other by their loops), each trying to make the other side lose its footing.

Depending on the village, one may expect the success either of the east team, which incarnates the masculine principle, or of the west team, incarnating the feminine principle, inferior to the first but guarantor of human fertility and the prosperity of the fields.

The houses, most of them made of wood, a few already of concrete, all face south and remain faithful to the traditional plan, mounted on pillars with the floor extending in front to form a narrow gallery running along the façade. That façade is wide open, except during typhoons, when it is protected by heavy wooden shutters. Each house contains two main rooms, the men's to the east, the women's to the west, with the kitchen in back, plus one or two small bedrooms for the children and supplies.

Each house also occupies the central part of a small garden enclosed by walls, usually built of coral rocks, which are cut into irregular polyhedrons. No mortar is used, but the rocks fit together as precisely as the stone blocks of Inca walls. Here and there, conglomerate walls are replacing them, and a third phase is beginning: walls made of fragments of conglomerate taken from demolitions.

Wherever the old coral walls survive, their color, darkened by age, forms an unforgettable harmony with the bright green grass carpeting asymmetrical little squares. The luxuriance of the foliage and flowers heralds the South Seas, and the pale and contorted roots of the ficus perform their work of destruction, dismantling the walls.

The layout of the gardens seems as invariable as the plan of the houses. On the south side, the outer wall makes way for an entrance; set back some-what, a small stone wall or a wood panel forming a screen protects domestic life from the gaze of pass-ersby, and especially from evil influences, which are also countered by magic formulas engraved or painted on boundary stones placed at the cross-roads. To enter the garden, you have to walk around the screen, either to the right or to the left. Use of the east side is reserved for ritual occasions; other-wise, everyone goes around to the west. Once you have crossed the threshold, you can head without hesitation to the northeast corner of the garden, where you are certain to see the altar of the deity of the place. Collected around it, at ground level or on a slight mound, are a few stones, shellfish, or other natural objects interesting for their form or rarity. On the west side, you know in advance where to find the pigsty (when it still exists) and the latrines, both placed under the protection of specialized gods.

In the kitchen, often incongruously modern between walls of bare boards, there is always a place for three stones, arranged in a small dish and representing *kamado*, the deity of the hearth. In the main room, a television set, turned on from morning till night even if no one is watching, is enough to persuade you that these "pictures of the floating world" in a new style occupy the place that formerly belonged to the *ukiyo-e* in Japan.

Women's Initiation Rites

I have just alluded to the local cults. Specialists insist on their archaism and believe they belong to a cultural stratum that may once have been common to all of Japan, prior to the formation of Shinto. What is striking about them, first and foremost, is the complete absence of temples or figurative representations. Despite the televisions, the electric stoves, the washing machines, I have never felt so close to prehistory as amid these coppices, these rocks, these caves, these natural wells, these springs, which for the people of the Ryukyu are the only expressions of the sacred, which, however, takes many forms.

In Greater Okinawa, covering some twenty kilometers around the Naha Prefecture, a ravaged nature — now occupied by empty barracks and American gasoline and equipment depots — attests to the violence of the battles of 1945. But on most of the island, the landscape seems intact or has gained the upper hand. Halfway across, on the Motobu Peninsula, the ruined wall surrounding Nakijin Castle, which in the fourteenth century was the site of an independent principality, looks like a miniature Great Wall of China. On a hill that remains a pilgrimage destination, rites were formerly celebrated facing the sea, in the direction of the Iheya and Izena Islands, from which ancestral navigators may have arrived. In any event, Iheya-jima is the birthplace of the first and second Shō Dynasties, which unified three earlier kingdoms and ruled the Ryukyu Islands from the fifteenth century until their annexation by Japan in 1879 (the Amami Islands to the north had been conquered by the lord of Satsuma in 1609).

On the other side of the island, to the southeast, on the Chinen Peninsula, the site of Seifa Utaki is still a place of veneration. It is a spectacular group of sheer rocks, crevices, and steep wooded slopes from which streams tumble down, and where you must beware of venomous snakes— plentiful enough, it appears, in all these islands for the inhabitants to dissuade you from going to seek ancient holy places that are too remote. From the peaks of Seifa Utaki, you perceive Kudaka-jima, which occupies a special place in the religious life of the Okinawa Islands. But every year, all the islands welcome in great pomp the gods from their *nira*, or *nirai*, dwelling place, located beyond the seas, who have come to bring human beings peace and good fortune.

It is well known that, notwithstanding institutions that are clearly patrilineal in orientation—for example, the *munchu*, an agnatic lineage with primarily a cult function—the entire religious life of the Ryukyu is in the women's hands. At the time of my visit, Kudaka-jima, with three hundred residents, counted no fewer than fifty-six priestesses, or *noro*, divided into hierarchical ranks. At the top of the pyramid, two principal priestesses, one for the east, one for the west, govern others who are responsible for the spiritual well-being of a greater or lesser number of households, depending on the priestess's order of importance. That system is founded, ideally, on the bond between brother and sister. He exercises secular authority; she ensures him and his household spiritual protection, thanks to the contact she maintains with the deities, but she can also curse him. All the same, in visiting these priestesses of various ranks—which we did all day long—it seemed to us that they had inherited their powers and their function either from their mother or from their mother-in-law. The priestess of a household or of a related group of households can therefore be, indiscriminately, a sister, a sister's daughter, a daughter, or a daughter-in-law, that is, a representative of the maternal line or of the paternal line, or a woman from a different lineage. Tōichi Mabuchi noted this thirty years ago; it is as if, for the indigenous mode of thought, the privilege of a relationship with the supernatural belonged to the female sex as such, rather than to a woman designated by her place in a determinate lineage.

The priestess's religious functions do not seem totally disinterested. The brother, the man or men of the household, theoretically have obligations toward her. Fishing for small fish, sea urchins, and shellfish among the rocks at low tide provides not insignificant dietary resources. The diligence with which the islanders went about this task reminded me of the saying of Indians on the Canadian coast, on the other side of the Pacific: "When the sea recedes, the table is set." And it is the priestesses who ritually control the biennial fishing for sea snakes, which are very dangerous and whose flesh is relished. The price reflects it: perhaps the priestesses take a profit. In any event, it seems clear that some great priestesses are rich compared to the average person and that they are not averse to displaying their wealth.

The practice of the cult remains humble and rustic, however. In Iheya and Izena, in remote woods or on the edges of villages, sometimes even in the courtyards of modern dwellings, we would spot *ashage:* small square or rectangular huts, their frames made of tree trunks and branches, supporting a high-pitched roof descending almost to the ground. To enter, you would have to bend over double; but in fact only the priestess goes in. It is there that, invisible to the eyes of the faithful, she communicates with the gods.

The priestesses, elderly for the most part, impose their authority with a natural gentility, a dignity free of all arrogance. Upon seeing or conversing with them, you have the impression that, for them-

selves and for others, their complicity with supernatural forces is a very simple thing that goes without saying, as it were. Nevertheless, they inspire
something more than deference in the men of the
village. Since early childhood, the males have
known that they are excluded from the rites that, to
assure them health and prosperity, their mothers,
sisters, daughters, or wives celebrate every month
(except October, a month without rites) in remote
places. The women bring back the leftovers of ceremonial meals, which the males of the house,
whatever their age, do not have the right to taste.

Men sometimes accede to the priesthood: in the
munchu, for example, where the brother becomes
his sister's assistant; or, when young, if they were
appointed by the priestesses to hunt sea snakes. But
in the maze of altars and holy places that occupy
the entire surface of the island (opposite the wharf
of Kudaka, a large sign warns visitors against the
sacrilege of moving even a stone), the old priest
serving as our guide showed us, with a mysterious
fear, the entrance to the sacred wood, where every
few years the women's initiation rites unfold. He
would not have risked setting foot there.

The same old man took us to beaches pounded
by the wind. It was there that the goddess Amami-

kyo, ancestor of the inhabitants of the Okinawa Islands, appeared on the eastern tip of the island. On the southern coast, divine messengers came bearing the five kinds of seeds with which the first fields were planted. Nothing about these sacred places attracts the attention of the visitor except, in each hollow of a rock, sticks of incense and coral rolling in the backwash, chosen and collected on the shore for their regular forms. These are the only offerings—and how primitive they are!—that decorate the makeshift altars. If the sands were to rise some day, future archaeologists, upon reaching the beach during their excavations, would wonder about the small piles of very polished pebbles, which I inspected with curiosity. How could they recognize them as amulets that, to protect the male members of each household, the priestesses came to seek on the beaches in February (three per beneficiary), and which they brought back in December? The sand blown by the wind would have quickly covered them.

Not far from there, our guide casually showed us the vestiges of an ancient shell mound. He explained that they were the remains of the first meals eaten by the goddess. And when I asked him where the seeds brought by the gods were first cultivated, he led us a few hundred meters into the interior to the little primordial field, *mifuda*, indicated by a stone altar. Not far away, a sort of swallow hole opened up. It is there that the goddess had retired to sleep. All this was narrated in a conversational tone. In the mind of our interlocutor, these events appeared to be a matter of course. They did not unfold in a mythic time but happened just yesterday. They are happening today, will happen tomorrow, since the gods who set foot there come back every year, and sacred rites and places prove their real presence over the entire surface of the island.

THE CRY OF THE MUTE PRINCE

This has been a very long preamble, but I could not omit it if I wanted to share with the reader something of the surprise caused me by an incident whose ambience I first had to reconstitute and whose background I had to supply.

Iheya-jima, with a population of about fifteen hundred, possesses what we would call a "community arts center" the like of which a European city of twenty thousand would not dare dream of: very vast, equipped with sophisticated audiovisual equipment, and, like all public places in Japan, kept in a state of meticulous cleanliness by women in white gloves. We shared one of the two inns on the island with laborers who worked at the port. A phone call came one evening from the community arts center, inviting us to a rehearsal of sacred songs in preparation for a yearly ceremony (after the session, we were allowed to see it recorded on video). When we arrived, almost no one was there, since the singers were all fishermen or farmers who, we were told, could not come until their workday was over. They appeared one by one, six or seven men and women, each carrying a *shamisen* with snake-skin stretched over its body, the traditional musical instrument of the region. Little by little, the chants rose up; someone whispered the translation to me. One song told the legend of a prince, mute from birth. Although he was the elder son, his father the king had decided to keep him from the throne because of his disability and to make his younger son his heir. A courtier attached to the person of the prince felt his master's humiliation so keenly that he sought to commit suicide. As he was about to carry out the deed, the mute suddenly recovered his speech and cried: "Stop!" Cured, he later succeeded his father.

Chanted by exotic peasants with slow solemnity

and a very generous melodic line, which was repeated several times, that narrative came as a shock to me. A short-circuit of memory made me recognize it as an episode from the life of Croesus, as Herodotus (1.38–39, 85) recounts it.

Croesus also had two sons: one was a deaf-mute from birth, who, Croesus said, "I count no son of mine"; the other he called "my only son," whom he lost. Apart from his disability, the surviving son was "a likely youth enough." During a war, "at the taking of the fortress a certain Persian, not knowing who Croesus was, came at him with intent to kill him . . . but this dumb son, seeing the Persian coming, in his fear and his grief broke into speech and cried, 'Man, do not kill Croesus!' This was the first word he uttered; and after that for all the days of his life he had power of speech."* Because his brother had died and he was himself cured, that son would have been doubly candidate for the throne, had his father been able to keep it.

Is this a fortuitous similarity between a Greek and a Japanese legend? That hypothesis is weak,

* *Herodotus*, translated by A. D. Godley, 4 vols. (Cambridge, Mass.: Harvard University Press 1957–1961), 1:47, 107, and 109.

especially since this is not a unique case. We need, of course, to take precautions in considering a Japanese narrative that, by virtue of its hero's name, Yuriwaka, and its plot, recall Odysseus and the *Odyssey* even in its details. Attested in Japan at the very beginning of the seventeenth century, the romance of Yuriwaka could have been inspired by the accounts of Portuguese traders or Spanish Jesuits (despite the very short interval between its appearance and the time when the plot of the *Odyssey* became well-known in the West, namely, the second half of the sixteenth century).* But we must not forget that the adventures of a hero that end with an archery competition constitute a theme of Asian origin, which is confirmed by the composite nature of Odysseus's bow, which stands out in the text of the *Odyssey* itself.† The question therefore remains open.

By contrast, there can be no doubt that the story of Midas was well known in the Far East from the Middle Ages on and probably well before. A Japa-

---

* E. L. Hibbard, "The Ulysses Motif in Japanese Literature," *Journal of American Folklore* 59, no. 233 (1946).

† H. L. Lorimer, *Homer and the Monuments* (London: Macmillan, 1950), pp. 298–300, 493–494.

nese historical work, compiled in the eleventh or twelfth centuries by an unknown author, alludes to "the man of old [who] dug a hole and talked into it" because he was bursting to tell a piece of news.*
A Korean chronicle from the thirteenth century, but which contained many elements dating back to archaic times,† recounts with even more embellishments than Ovid a story in which King Kyongmun, who reigned from 861 to 875, met the same fate as Midas:

> One morning when the King awoke, he discovered that his two ears had grown overnight into long furry ones like those of a donkey. . . . He was compelled to cover his head with a sort of turban . . . so that nobody ever knew his secret except the tailor who made the turban. He, of course, was given the strictest orders to tell nobody.
>
> Faithful servant of the King though he was, the

---

* Helen C. McCullough, *Okagami: The Great Mirror, a Study and Translation* (Princeton: Princeton University Press, 1980), p. 65.

† Iryŏn, *Samguk Yusa: Legends and History of the Three Kingdoms of Ancient Korea*, translated by Ha Tae-Hung and Grafton K. Mintz (N.p.[Rockville, Md.]: Silk Pagoda, 2006), p. 106.

tailor was continually tormented by his inability
to speak of this strange and unique event. Finally
he became ill and was obliged to go for a rest to
Torim Temple on the outskirts of Kyonju. One
day he came out into the back garden of his temple alone and unattended . . . Seeing that no-one
was within earshot, he plunged suddenly into a
bamboo grove nearby and shouted repeatedly at
the top of his voice, "My King has long ears like a
donkey!" Then, having at last won peace of
mind, he fell dead on the spot.

Ever afterward, when the wind blew through
this particular bamboo grove, the sound it made
seemed to say "My King has long ears like a donkey." . . . At last it reached the King's long ears.
He . . . ordered the bamboos cut down and palms
planted in their place. This was done and the
palms grew rapidly. But when the wind blew
through them they sang "My King has long
ears . . ." dropping the last three words.

. . . Torim-sa fell into decay. But new shoots
grew up from the roots of the bamboos which
had been cut down and people took cuttings to
plant in their gardens so that they could hear the
song they sang, and they did likewise with the
palms.

Versions of the Midas story proliferated in the folklore of Mongolia and Tibet.* Their possible arrival in Korea and Japan is not problematic. There is therefore no reason to think that the presence of the story of Croesus on the Okinawa Islands poses a problem either. Buddhism, which incorporated so many Hellenic and Hellenistic elements, could have brought motifs originating in Greece to the Far East. Or perhaps the homeland of the protagonists — Lydia in one case, Phrygia in the other — is a clue that the two narratives have their point of origin in Asia, from which they could have traveled in both directions.

---

* R. A. Stein, *Recherches sur l'épopée et le barde au Tibet* (Paris: PUF, 1959), pp. 381–383, 411–412.

Photo by Junzo Kawada. Copyright © 2011 Éditions du Seuil, "La Librairie du XXIe siècle."

Photo by Machiko Ogawa. Copyright © 2011 Éditions du Seuil, "La Librairie du XXIe siècle."

5

Sengai

The Art of Accommodating Oneself to the World

THE ART OF Sengai, as André Malraux realized, leaves the Western beholder perplexed: "No other Far Eastern art," he said, "is so remote from our own and from us."

Every time the meaning of the legends that Sengai inscribed in the margins of his paintings is revealed to us, we grasp a little better the reasons for that lack of understanding. By their meaning and their graphics, the words have as much importance as the painted subject. Because these short texts, often in the form of poems, with their implicit quotations, facetious allusions, and hidden meanings escape us, we have only a fragmented perception of the works.

In a sense, however, that is true as well for all Far Eastern painting, which is indissociable from calligraphy, and not only because calligraphy almost always occupies a place in it. Each thing represented—tree, rock, waterway, path, mountain—acquires, beyond its sensible appearance, a philosophical meaning, by virtue of the way the painter depicts it and situates it in an organized whole.

Even if we confine ourselves to calligraphy, it is clear that, despite all the translators' efforts, the essence of *haikai* poetry—that of Bashō, for example, to whom Sengai felt close—remains beyond our reach. What counts as much as the literal meaning, the only accessible one, is the choice of one character rather than another to express the same idea, as well as the style of writing (the manuals distinguish at least five) and the layout of the text on the sheet. That is particularly true for Sengai, whose cursive line, bold simplifications, and rapid and casual brushstroke abolish the distance between figuration and writing.

One problem persists for the Western art lover. It is the purity, elegance, sobriety, and rigor of Japanese art that initially touched us. In addition, to confine myself to a single example, we are obliged to wonder—since Sengai is the exact contemporary of Kiyonaga, Utamaro, and Eishi, painters of feminine grace and beauty—at the coexistence, during the same era and in the same country, of forms of expression that are very remote from each other. Perhaps they have a distant and common origin in the painted scrolls of the eleventh and twelfth centuries, in which the properly Japanese gift for concision, the art of saying the most with the least, took hold. To evaluate Sengai's art, we must look at it from other angles as well.

The first, immediately apparent aspect, which is nevertheless not superficial, could be the penchant for playfulness, which I see as one of the components of the Japanese spirit. I am not thinking only of contemporary kinds of play (*pachinko*, golf, karaoke); or even of parlor games, which from the Heian period on had such a large place in court life and literary romances. I am thinking quite simply of playthings and amusing objects where the inventor's ingenuity shows through.

I was often struck in Japan by the fascination exerted on very serious bankers or businessmen by innocent toys, for which their European counterparts would feel or feign indifference. I was therefore not surprised—was delighted, rather—when, on his first visit, a distinguished individual handed me with great fanfare an object representing a caged bird, which chirped every time you happened to cut off an electric beam powered by a battery hidden in the base.

Japan may be beholden to that playful spirit for its victory over all its rivals in the field of microelectronics. That may also explain the extravagant architectural constructions, designed in the most heterogeneous styles, that can be seen rising up here and there in the cities.

In the graphic arts, that playfulness emerged very early on in the famous scrolls attributed to the twelfth-century painter and monk Toba Sōjō: satirical animal representations, which founded a tradition that Hokusai revived during Sengai's own lifetime. Twenty or thirty years later, Kuniyoshi's caricatural prints with human or animal subjects still echoed that tradition.

It is true that, even in the case of the old painter, these whimsical figures appear to have been inspired by social criticism and not by a religious spirit, as they were in Sengai. But the demarcation line is not easy to draw. Toba was a monk; and though in the late seventeenth century the great painter Kōrin, who achieved considerable social success, produced lighthearted, humorous works, we cannot forget that his younger brother and collaborator, Kenzan, was an adherent of Zen. To grasp the connection, we must dig deeper.

EMANCIPATING ONESELF FROM DUALISM

By virtue of his association with Zen, Sengai is situated within the spiritual tradition of the masters of the tea ceremony, who, from the sixteenth century on, sought the crudest and most humble utensils in Korea and China: poor peasants' rice bowls, made on site by village artisans. The fact that they were produced without manual skill or aesthetic pretensions conferred more value on them in the eyes of the tea masters than if they had been true works of art. That marked the birth of the taste for rough materials, irregular forms, what one tea master called, using an expression that earned him many followers, the "art of the imperfect." In that respect, the Japanese are the true inventors of "primitivism," which the West would rediscover several centuries later, through African and Oceanic arts, popular objects, naïve art, and in a different way, the ready-made—but significantly, only after passing through the stage of Japonism.

Unlike the Western aesthete, the tea masters were not concerned with restoring the freedom of the creative gesture prior to conventional rules, or with inventing a mode of expression situated beyond a "know-how" that had fallen into banalities (as in raku ceramic, where, through intentional distortions, the overly conscious pursuit of the imperfect became a style; in the graphic arts, the West provides an equivalent of sorts with the monotype). Rather, they sought to emancipate themselves from any dualism, in order to achieve a state where the opposition between the beautiful and the ugly no longer has any meaning. Buddhism calls that state "thusness," an existence prior to all distinctions, impossible to define except as being thus.

It is not out of place to invoke that philosophy of pottery with respect to Sengai, who was a potter and ceramics decorator in his leisure time. And as a painter, he did not propose to attain beauty by eliminating ugliness. "Do not discriminate the refined from the crude," said a Chinese patriarch of Zen in the sixth century, "there is no need to choose." It would be wrong to see that spontaneous graphics, free of all constraints and all rules, where carelessness and elegance combine, as something resembling caricature. Caricature intentionally exaggerates and deforms reality, whereas an art like Sengai's results from the impromptu encounter between reality and a gesture. The work does not imitate a model. It celebrates the coincidence, or better, the fusion, of two fleeting phenomena: a form, an expression, or an attitude, and the impetus given to the brush. In its way, Zen painting expresses the essence of Buddhist thought, which denies any permanent reality to beings and things, and aspires through Enlightenment to a state where distinctions between existence and nonexistence, life and death, emptiness and fullness, self and other, and the beautiful and the ugly are abolished; by virtue of the same principles, any means for achieving that state is legitimate. Zen does not establish a hierarchy of values between transcendental meditation, puns, and derision.

There is nothing surprising, therefore, about a religious painter being funny. Zen literature abounds in comic little stories such as the one evoked in one of Sengai's paintings. A blind man illuminates himself with a lantern at night. People are surprised: "It's so I won't get knocked down," he explains. Nevertheless, he is. It is pointed out to him that his lantern has gone out; he relights it. Knocked down again, he takes the culprit to task. "But I'm blind," the other replies.

The laughter provoked by that tale comes as a

result of a short-circuit between two semantic fields. Blindness shifts unexpectedly from a term value to a function value. A mental jolt thus puts the listener on the path of Enlightenment, leading him to understand that empirical existence confines us within contradictions and that it is pointless to believe we will be able to escape them through multiple precautions.

The roots of that oblique pedagogy are ancient. The school traces it back to Buddha: in answer to one of his disciples, his only response was to make a gesture that appeared incomprehensible to them and on which they meditated tirelessly. Perhaps the role played by Sanskrit literature must also be acknowledged, since it makes systematic use of wordplay, homonyms, because double meanings oblige one to break the empirical connections between phenomena and provide access to supersensible reality. More obviously, the role of Taoism must be noted: profoundly rooted in the spirit of the people, it displays its contempt for social conventions and, like Buddhism, rejects all forms of dualism.

In China, these cross-influences gave rise to Ch'an, which stemmed from the Indian practice of meditation (*dhyāna*); then, in Japan, they produced

Zen, which monks who had visited China introduced in the twelfth century, along with the Chinese technique of monochrome wash painting, which became a vogue among the literati.

Sengai has his place in that lineage. Twenty-seven patriarchs of contemplative Buddhism followed in succession in India. In the sixth century, the twenty-eighth, Bodhidharma ("Daruma" in Japanese), transported it to China. Six centuries later, the Japanese monk Eisai (Yosai) established Zen in northern Kyushu. Sengai became his successor after another six centuries.

It is well known that Zen as a whole declares that tradition, doctrine, and sacred texts are without value: "To read them is as pointless as trying to get rid of dust by sweeping with a broom," Sengai wrote on one painting. The only things that count are one's inner life and the practice of meditation. Of these practices, the Rinzai branch (to which Sengai belonged) represents the extreme form, excluding all communication between master and disciple except inarticulate cries, interjections devoid of meaning, and brutality: blows with sticks or fists, intended to break the disciple's mental equilibrium, to plunge him into mental chaos, which might serve as a trigger to illumination.

Several of Sengai's paintings evoke responses, or refusals to respond, that have remained famous. For example, a disciple who had asked, "Do dogs also have a Buddha Nature?" received by way of reply a flat refusal, expressed in a monosyllable. The wording of the question implied that there could be living beings on one hand, a Buddha Nature on the other, a duality challenged by Buddhism. To a disciple who wondered whether he could contemplate without blasphemy the Buddha while sweeping, the master, it is said, indirectly gave him to understand that that activity was profoundly religious—like all manual labor, in fact—since the Buddha, present to our gaze in all things, is also so in dust.

Above all, Rinzai makes systematic use of koans, questions or riddles posed in contradictory terms—the classic example is "What is the sound of one hand clapping?"—which create a roadblock in the mind and oblige it to seek a way out in a dimension external to rational thought. For weeks or months, the disciple will have to devote himself to that "contemplation of the word" (a Rinzai definition), speculate to the point of exhaustion on a meaning that cannot be found, confronting an intellectual violence that corresponds on a different plane to the physical and verbal violence to which he is also subjected.

Let me make a digression. In France, the academic tradition does not completely eschew the koan. A student, later a renowned writer, was abruptly asked during a competitive exam: "Who did what when?" Refusing to be nonplussed, the candidate responded at once: "In 410 Alaric took Rome and sacked it." He passed with honors. Thirteen centuries earlier, in China, the sixth Ch'an patriarch had formulated a koan in almost the same terms. "What is it?" he asked his disciple suddenly, who retorted: "It, what's that?" and obtained a certificate of succession.

That little apologue is a good illustration of the difference between the Western spirit and Buddhism. For the Westerner, a seeker of his own nature, there is no question to which he cannot or ought not to find an answer: the scientific spirit is there in embryo. That smugness is countered by Buddhist wisdom. No question can receive an answer, since each one calls for another question. Nothing possesses a nature of its own; the so-called realities of the world are fleeting. They follow in succession and mingle together; they cannot be captured in the mesh of a definition.

A painting by Sengai also cannot be said to be finished. Each expresses the brief moment that the brush took to trace its line. The work has a form more temporal than spatial, one so inconsistent, as Sengai well knows, that he repeats many versions of the same themes. There are practically no isolated works by Sengai, only series. In the same way, for Buddhism, the apparent individuality of each thing or being is resolved in a series (*samtāna*) of physical, biological, or psychological phenomena, precariously united. They follow in succession, combine, and repeat one another. In such an art, the painting does not exist as an object, as it does for us: it is something that happens and then vanishes behind another, equally fleeting painting.

Some would be tempted to link that conception of the work of art to Western notions that give priority to the creative gesture. In fact, it is the exact opposite. The abstract painter, especially of "lyric" genres, seeks to express his personality in his work; by contrast, the Zen monk aspires to be the insubstantial place where something of the world finds expression through him.

I have already pointed out the importance of calligraphy, and not only because of its value as a text: it is an integral part of the work. In the painting representing a willow tree, two characters form the word "endurance": the first, *kan*, very black and thick, seems to convey the violence of the wind; the second, *nin*, lighter in color and with a thinner line, would appear to signify the flexibility of the tree, whose movement is replicated by the lower part of the character. In the well-known representation of the cosmos by means of a circle, a triangle, and a square, vertical calligraphy plays an indispensable role, balancing out the horizontal block formed by the three figures.

The painting overall thus realizes synchronically the effect of orthogonal totality, which results, less directly, from a reading of the painting from right to left, the order in which the figures were drawn, from circle to square. Elsewhere, image and writing form a two-part counterpoint. For example, only an allusion in the text makes it possible to link the kettle to the legend of the drunken ogre Shutendoji, who was put to sleep with drugged sake. The series that Sengai devoted to the poet Bashō illustrates in an extraordinarily subtle manner a dialectical interplay between the image and the written word. Indeed, although the text replaces Bashō with the frog from one of his most famous haiku—that is, the creature stands in for the creator—the drawing renders Bashō physically present in the form of a banana tree (the poet's name and that of the plant are the same). Drawing and text, inseparable, echo each other through the complementary voices of metaphor and metonymy.

Another remarkable aspect of these rapid and apparently sloppy drawings is their documentary precision. However cursory the indications, nothing is missing, and everywhere the line becomes sign. Each deity is recognizable by his attributes: Jizō holds his sistrum; Fudo Myōō has his distinctive hairstyle and, as is only right, he is cross-eyed and his canine teeth stick out. The sketchy masks of the deities who pulled the sun goddess from her cave are the same ones that, even today, the peasant actors of Kyushu wear to perform that scene, near the place where, according to legend, it unfolded. And the plum tree not only adorns Sugawara no Michizane's sleeve: the blossoming tree clings to his body, as if to better show that it has magically rejoined that exiled minister, inconsolable at having had to leave the garden that was his pride and joy.

Tags and Calligraphy

It is a misuse of language to bestow the name "calligraphy" on the art of certain contemporary non-figurative painters. The pseudo-signs they produce have no intrinsic meaning prior to their reuse by the artist. (In present-day France, only the authors of what are known as "tags," inscriptions legible for the initiated on the walls and cars of the metro, would deserve to be called calligraphers.) Written signs, which already have a social existence, acquire an individual existence by passing through the calligrapher's hand. The legend of Kōbōdaishi, "the five-brush monk," grand master of calligraphy, even asserts that these signs become living beings.

By means of signs that are not signs, Western lyrical abstraction claims to objectify the self: the movement that drives it is centrifugal. For calligraphy, as for Zen painting, the self is the means by which the sign expresses itself and, secondarily, takes in hand the scriptor's individuality.

That opposition between the centrifugal and the centripetal, that contrast between the West and Japan, can also be found in other realms, from the structure of the Japanese language, which places the subject last, to manual labor: how the saw and plane are manipulated, how the potter's wheel is engaged, how a needle is threaded, cloth stitched, and so on. In all these realms, the Japanese artisan favors movements in the opposite direction of our own. Zen painting also displays that trait, which is among the most typical of the spirit of Japan.

That painting also coincides with the concrete realities of Japanese life, though by different paths. Zen is a practice of meditation that is supposed to lead to wisdom, and that wisdom consists of freeing oneself from the world of appearances. Even so, wisdom, having reached its ultimate stage, discovers that, a prisoner to other illusions, it must be wary of itself as well. Yet a knowledge that doubts itself is no longer knowledge. The attainment of that supreme knowledge, that everything is unknowledge, liberates the sage. At the point he has reached, that amounts to knowing that nothing has meaning and to sharing, as if everything had a meaning, the existence of his peers as an ordinary man.

That explains the informal, good-natured side of Sengai's work. A little theater of the world, it offers a detailed portrayal, precious to the ethnologist, of Japanese life and society in his time. Everything is there: from the Buddhist pantheon, the saints of

Zen hagiography, the heroes of legends, and the characters from traditional folklore, to the scenes of daily life, local landscapes, occupations—including those of beggar and prostitute—animals, plants, cultivation of the earth, household utensils. Were it not for his profane inspiration, they would bring to mind Hokusai's *Manga*, equally rich, varied, and full of verve; and even more, I daresay, despite the distance between the genres, the times, and the places, Montaigne's *Essays*, comparable in their scope and their vivacity to Sengai's works, written as well as painted. Indeed, Montaigne's mode of thought probably offers the most points of contact in the West with Buddhism.

That connection attests to the universal import of lessons that arose in different eras, at opposite ends of the Eurasian continent. They likewise incite us to seek, in the rejection of appearances, in the skepticism toward all beliefs, and in the renunciation of attaining an ultimate truth, the state that best befits the sage: that of living serenely among his peers, sharing their little joys, sympathizing with their sorrows, and accommodating himself to the world.

6

Domesticating Strangeness

For it was between things most opposed that friendship was chiefly to be found, since everything desired its opposite, not its like.
Plato, *Lysis*, 215e, trans. W. R. M. Lamb

THE WEST discovered Japan twice: in the mid-sixteenth century, when the Jesuits entered it, having come in the wake of the Portuguese merchants (they were expelled in the next century); and three hundred years later, with the naval action the United States conducted to compel the Empire of the Rising Sun to open its doors to international trade.

Father Luís Fróis was one of the principal protagonists in the first discovery. In the second, a comparable role fell to the Englishman Basil Hall Chamberlain, for whom Fróis now appears to have been the precursor. Born in 1850, Chamberlain visited Japan, settled there, and became a professor at the University of Tokyo. In one of his books, *Things*

Japanese (1890), written in the form of a dictionary, an entry under "T," "Topsy-Turvydom," develops the idea that "the Japanese do many things in a way that runs directly counter to European ideas of what is natural and proper."

For example, Japanese seamstresses threaded their needles by pushing the eye onto the thread, instead of pushing the thread into the eye. They also pricked the fabric on the needle rather than sticking the needle into the fabric, as we do.

An object in modeled terra cotta, recently exhumed during archaeological excavations, attests that, as far back as the sixth century, the Japanese mounted their horses from the right, contrary to our custom. Even today, foreign visitors are astonished that the Japanese carpenter saws by pulling the tool toward him and not by pushing it away as we do; and that he manipulates in the same way the "drawknife," a two-handled knife used for planing and thinning out wood. In Japan, the potter sets the wheel in motion with his left foot, clockwise, unlike the European or Chinese potter, who sets it in motion with his right foot, counterclockwise.

These practices, as the Jesuit missionary had already noted, do not merely differentiate Japan from Europe: the demarcation line passes between insular Japan and continental Asia. Along with many other elements of its culture, Japan borrowed from China the crosscut saw, which cuts by pushing; but from the fourteenth century on, saws that cut by pulling, invented in Japan itself, supplanted the Chinese model. And the drawknife that is pushed, which came from China in the sixteenth century, gave way a hundred years later to models that the user pulls toward himself.

Most of these examples are already briefly cited by Chamberlain. Had he been able to read Fróis's treatise, discovered eleven years after his death, he would have found a fascinating repertoire of observations, sometimes identical to his own, but more numerous, and all leading to the same conclusion.

Neither Chamberlain nor Fróis probably had any notion that they were expressing their views of Japan in the same terms that Herodotus, in the fifth century B.C.E., used for a country, Egypt, which he saw as no less marked by mystery. The Greek traveler wrote that the Egyptians behave in all things contrary to other peoples. The women engage in trade while the men remain at home. It is the men and not the women who weave; and they begin the weft at the bottom of the loom, not at the top as in other countries. The women urinate standing up, the men squat. And so on. I shall not continue the list, which demonstrates a mental attitude common to the three authors.

It is not always possible to see the disparities they enumerate as contradictions. These disparities often have a more modest status: sometimes mere differences, sometime presence in one place, absence in the other. Fróis was not unaware of this, since he placed the words *contradições* and *diferenças* side by side in the title of his book. And yet for him, even more than for the other two authors, there was clearly an effort to make all the contrasts fit the same mold. Hundreds of comparisons, formulated concisely and as parallel constructions, suggest that Fróis was not just pointing out differences, but rather that all these oppositions actually constitute inversions. When Herodotus, Fróis, and Chamberlain considered the practices of two civilizations, one exotic and the other domestic, they all had the same ambition. Moving beyond mutual unintelligibility, they insisted on bringing to light transparent relationships of symmetry.

Was that not a way of recognizing that Egypt for Herodotus, and Japan for Fróis and Chamberlain, possessed a civilization equal to their own in every way? The recognition of a symmetry between two cultures unites them, even as it places them in opposition. They appear both similar and different, the symmetrical image of ourselves reflected in a mirror, an image irreducible to us, even though we find ourselves in every detail. When the traveler convinces himself that practices in complete opposition to his own, which by that very fact he would be tempted to despise and reject with disgust, are in reality identical to them when viewed in reverse, he provides himself with the means to domesticate strangeness, to make it familiar to himself.

In pointing out that the practices of the Egyptians and those of his compatriots were in a relation of systematic inversion, Herodotus actually placed them on the same level and indirectly accounted for the role that the Greeks assigned to Egypt: a civilization of a respectable antiquity, a depository of an esoteric knowledge from which lessons could still be learned.

Similarly, but in different eras, Fróis and Chamberlain, placed in comparable circumstances vis-à-vis another civilization, also appealed to symmetry: Fróis, without being aware of it, since it was not yet time; and Chamberlain, with full awareness of what he was doing. They provided us with a means for better understanding the deep-seated reason for which, in about the mid-nineteenth century, the West acquired the sense that it was rediscovering itself in the forms of aesthetic and poetic sensibility that Japan was proposing.

7

The Shameless Dance of Ame no Uzume

THE ANALOGIES between the shameless dance of Ame no Uzume on one hand, that of Iambe in the Homeric hymn to Demeter and of Baubo according to Clement of Alexandria on the other, are too well known for me to revisit them. It was quickly noticed that a similar analogy exists for a romance from ancient Egypt, translated and published in about 1930. The resemblance is so striking that an Orientalist, Isidore Lévy, proposed at the time to see it as the distant origin of the Japanese narrative.

Within the context of this colloquium, the Egyptian romance has a particular interest, because an ape god plays a role in it. I shall examine it from that angle, notwithstanding the considerable interval of time that separates it from the *Kojiki* and the *Nihongi*. The Egyptian romance is known to us through a papyrus dating to the end of the second millennium B.C.E., and specialists believe that the first written text goes back to the Middle Kingdom, about a thousand years earlier.

The romance begins when the gods, holding court, are unable to decide between the two pretenders to succeed the great god Osiris: Horus, Osiris's young son, ardently supported by his mother, Isis; and Seth, the maternal uncle of Horus. Pre-Harakhti, the sun god, who presides over the tribunal, is inclined to favor Seth against the general opinion, which is favorable to Horus. He is therefore the object of an offensive remark from Baba, the ape god. Insulted, Pre-Harakhti retreats to his pavilion, where he spends the whole day lying on his back, his heart heavy. After a long time, his daughter Hathor appears. She lifts her dress and reveals her genitals. At that sight, the great god laughs, gets up, and returns to sit on the tribunal.

The resemblance to the Japanese narratives is compelling, not only because the offended deity is the Sun in both cases but also because of the decisive function attributed to laughter (whether that of the deity himself, of the dancer, or of the spectators). Herodotus (2.106, 102) declares he had seen the monuments representing female sex organs that Pharaoh Sesostris III, whose era corresponds approximately to that of the first written version of the romance, erected in Syria and Palestine to jeer at the enemies he had defeated. Herodotus also recounts (2.60) that even in his own time (that is, fifteen hundred years later), men and women taking boats to the festival of Bubastis, whenever they came alongside a city, navigated as close to the bank as possible; the women on the boat ridiculed those of the city, got on their feet, and lifted their robes. The comical connotation of female exhibitionism thus seems to have been a constant of Egyptian civilization over the centuries.

An ape god assumes the place occupied in Japan by Susanoo, as offender of the sun god responsible for his retreat. That leads us to wonder about the connotations of the ape (in this case, the baboon, *Papio hamadryas*) among the ancient Egyptians. In their view, a secret sympathy united apes and the movements of celestial bodies. Apes had a special affinity for the planet Mercury (the one closest to the sun). A chorus of baboons greeted the appearance of the sun bark at dawn. It was believed that apes urinated abundantly during equinoxes, and it was said they were responsible for the phases of the moon: joyous when it was full, bereaved when it was new. The same close relationship between apes and astronomical or meteorological phenomena existed in India: Hanuman was the son of the wind god. He is also found in Central America among the Mayas (who saw apes as human beings who had been transformed by the wind) and in South America.

To assign the sense of "ape" to the morpheme *saru* in the name of the Japanese god Saruta-hiko is to choose one hypothesis among others. But that god also plays the role of intermediary between the celestial and terrestrial worlds. A formidable deity (like Hanuman), he might have stood in the way of the gods' descent, but laughter and a second dance by Ame no Uzume cheered him up and persuaded him to lead their march to the east.

It is noteworthy that that dual function, first on a vertical and then on a horizontal axis, was also attributed to the ape by European iconology during the Middle Ages, where the feminine form of the animal's Latin name was usually used. By contrast, in Japanese mythology simian nature is, so to speak, incarnated in the male and female couple formed by Saruta-hiko and Ame no Uzume. According to art historians, the presence, enigmatic at first glance, of an ape in paintings depicting the Annunciation supposedly serves to contrast the first (sinful) Eve to the new Eve (the Virgin Mary), signifying the shift from the Old Testament to the New. In medieval iconography, therefore, the ape may be a symbol of the fall of humankind; in Japan, conversely, it is associated with the descent of the gods and has a positive value. Its role is transitional in both cases, as confirmed in Japan by the affinity between Saruta-hiko and Kōshin, god of roads.

An Old Beggar Woman

In what may be called the Izumo cycle, which follows the account of Susanoo's expulsion from the celestial world, the *Kojiki* introduces an episode called "The Hare of Inaba," the interpretation of which has left commentators perplexed. We know it reproduces a tale, widespread from India to the Celebes Islands (Klaus Antoni has compiled the different versions of it), in which the role of the victim is also played by a crocodile.

Some, to be sure, have disputed whether the word *wani* could have designated the crocodile, an animal unknown to the Japanese of ages past because it does not exist in their country. But could they not have had an indirect knowledge of it? Archaic China made the crocodile the inventor of the drum and of musical harmony. The belief survives in latent form at least in Burma, where traditional lutes are shaped like crocodiles. The fact that the word *wani* in Japan composes part of the name of certain wooden or metal gongs is enough to suggest that familiarity with the crocodile in its mythical form had extended that far.

I myself have identified mythical narratives very close to the story of the hare of Inaba in North and South America. That vast diffusion makes its presence in Japan less surprising. But it is still intriguing that a little southeast Asian tale about the quarrels between two animals, apparently designed to amuse an audience, could have found its place in a grandiose mythology.

It is therefore worthwhile to note that an episode of the same kind appears in the Egyptian romance and that, there again, it follows the emergence of the Sun from the retreat where he had shut himself up, after another god (the ape Baba, in what would become Susanoo's role) offended him. Here is that episode:

Exasperated by Isis's interventions in favor of her son Horus, Seth demands that the proceedings go on in her absence. The tribunal agrees, moves to the Island of the Middle, and orders the ferryman, named Anti, not to allow any women on his bark. But Isis assumes the appearance of a poor old lady, persuades the ferryman that the prohibition does not apply to her, and buys his complaisance with a gold ring. Upon reaching the island, she changes into a ravishing girl, who arouses Seth's passion. Through a clever ruse, she leads him to recognize the injustice of his claim to the throne.

Once again, a duped ferryman is at issue, but here he is not a crocodile. Anti, "the clawed one," is represented as a falcon. Nevertheless, the saurian can be made out in the background: in the city named after Anti, where the battle unfolds between Seth and Isis and Horus (which brings us back to our story), Plutarch relates that someone saw an old woman lying with a crocodile (*De sollertia animalium* 23.9).

The hieroglyphic name of the city was pronounced "city of the sandal" because Antee (that is, Anti) had lost the city of Aphroditopolis, on the other bank of the Nile, which was called "city of the two sandals." That loss of a sandal can therefore be linked to the punishment inflicted on Anti for having transported Isis: according to the text, "the front part of his feet" was cut off, a punishment curiously similar to that of Susanoo, whose nails were torn from his hands and feet.

The form the romance gives to the ferryman episode has led the Hellenist Jean Hubaux to integrate it into a larger whole, known in Greece through two other examples, in which a goddess, Hera or Aphrodite, turns into an old beggar woman to test the charity of a ferryman. Transported free of cost, the goddess rewards him by giving him youth and beauty, or, in the case of Jason, by making him lose a sandal (which, for reasons that would take too long to recall here, will lead to his capture of the Golden Fleece). By contrast, Anti proscribes gold in his city because, corrupted by the gift of a ring made from that metal, he lost part of his feet as punishment. Analogies, connections, relations of symmetry or inversion can be vaguely perceived between the Greek and Egyptian narratives and between the Egyptian and Japanese narratives. Do they allow us to infer that these traditions were in contact with and mutually influenced each other? On the contrary, careful consideration leads us to be cautious.

Let us not forget, in the first place, that nearly three thousand years separate the *Kojiki* from the

Egyptian romance. Comparatists are too often tempted to span millennia, to join together the end and the beginning, as if nothing had happened in these enormous intervals, simply because we know nothing about them. But there is no justification for imagining that the millennia whose history is unknown to us were less rich in upheavals, ruptures, and events than the others. We must therefore be wary of assuming links of filiation or borrowings between works very remote in time or space, unless, of course, we can produce independent proof of them.

In the second place, the *Kojiki* and the Egyptian romance are not myths but literary creations, each attributable to an author, known or unknown, who exploited mythic subject matter while arranging it in his own way. And these works have very different, even opposing characteristics: one is an epic account pervaded by the supernatural and placed in the service of dynastic claims; the other is a humorous tale that makes fun of the gods to amuse an audience.

Nevertheless, the themes and motifs mysteriously echo one another. They likely belong to an archaic mythological stratum. That in no way implies that genealogical relationships can be established between their manifestations. The modern form of systematics of the animal kingdom, known as *cladism*, has taught us to distinguish primitive from derived characteristics. It is not possible to conclude, based on the presence of primitive characteristics in common, that two species are closely related. The human being cannot be linked to the tortoise or salamander simply because they all have five digits. That is a primitive characteristic that was probably shared by all land vertebrates. A few species retained it, others lost it: for example, the horse, to which, despite its single digit, human beings are closer than to any batrachian or reptile.

If we transpose that distinction to mythology, we may say that the primitive characteristics of myths consist of mental operations that are formal in their essence. In the present case, it is sufficient that mythic thought conceive the idea of a longitudinal journey, like that of the sun from east to west, for the idea to arise, via inversion, of a transverse journey, like that of a ferryman from one bank of a waterway to the other, or from one side of an inlet to the other.

Other conceptual inversions, triggered by the

first, may come to enrich the tableau. The idea of a heavenly longitudinal journey that is interrupted gives rise to that of an earthly longitudinal journey that is established or reestablished. Let us go a step further: if the first longitudinal journey, in heaven, is interrupted, whereas later, the continuity of the second journey, the one on earth, is assured (the respective roles assigned in Japan to Susanoo and Saruta-hiko are recognizable here), the transverse journey, on water, must not be brutally prevented or graciously offered, but rather—this is an intermediate solution—obtained through haggling, ruse, or deceit. That explains, in terms of a purely logical necessity, why the ferryman motif can appear next to that of the offended sun in two texts so remote in other respects.

The Egyptian Seth and Susanoo

These primitive characteristics, virtually present everywhere, are not always actualized. The *Kojiki* organizes the mythic subject matter available to it with such perfection that, when the first translations appeared in Europe, a few scholars did not hesitate to see them as the most faithful reflection

to have reached us of the great primordial myth
—*Urmythus*, as the Germans said—formerly common to humankind as a whole. And in fact, its
author clearly perceived that an image of the transverse journey had to have its place in the array of
transformations. To fill that slot, he took what he
had at hand: a little animal tale. This is a fine example of *bricolage*, the operative mode in mythic
thought. The compilers of the *Nihongi*, scholars
rather than poets, did not feel the same need, or
they adopted a critical attitude toward the tale of
the hare of Inaba. They thus ignored it or intentionally excluded it.

I shall attempt to show briefly that the chapter
from the *Kojiki* and the original tale from southeast Asia are united by a characteristic that cladism
would call derived—one that belongs properly to
them, isolates them from apparently neighboring
forms, and establishes their kinship on a real foundation.

Theoretically, two solutions are available to anyone wishing to cross a body of water or an arm of
the sea: one is mobile, a ferryman; the other im-
mobile, a bridge. Myths generally choose between
them. In the Americas, for example, the duped ani-

mal can serve as a bridge: it is then a wading bird, never a crocodile. Or it can serve as a ferryman: it is then a crocodile (an alligator or caiman in the Americas) and not a bird. Yet the Japanese and southeast Asian versions have a common trait that distinguishes them from all the others: they bring about a synthesis of the two solutions. The crocodile, in becoming plural, is transformed from a solitary ferryman into a bridge.

Similarly, the gigantic size, the terrible and demoniacal aspect, and the extraordinary powers that the *Nihongi* attributes to Saruta-hiko are common only to him and to the Indian king of the apes, Hanuman. These traits alone make it possible to declare their real kinship.

We must therefore be wary of too remote comparisons. Certain similarities have to do not with historical or prehistorical relationships but with what could be called elementary structures of mythic thought. Their occurrence in both places does not mean that genealogical connections exist between one or another of their manifestations, but only that they sometimes come to the surface, all together or in fragments. They can also remain unexpressed; in some cases, they may have simply disappeared. It is within such a perspective that, it seems to me, we need to consider the similarities between the Egyptian romance and the Japanese mythic narratives.

Although we must consider the similarities with reservations, the differences may serve as food for thought. From one work to the other, the characters correspond and permutate into a single function. The Egyptian Seth and the Japanese Susanoo take turns in the role of the impetuous and formidable deity, destined to become the god of storms, one in the sky, near the sun, the other on earth or in the subterranean world, after being cast out of the community of the gods. It falls to Ame no Uzume to reestablish or facilitate two journeys in opposite directions, first in heaven, then on land. In the Egyptian romance, Hathor resorts to the same means as the Japanese goddess to reestablish a single journey, which nevertheless remains ambiguous: symbolically celestial but earthly at the literal level of the narrative. The function of interrupting the heavenly journey is performed in Japan by Susanoo, in Egypt by an ape god; by contrast, in Japan, his counterpart performs exactly the opposite function. That invites us to wonder about the relationship that might exist between these two re-doubtable deities from the most ancient Japanese pantheon, Susanoo and Saruta-hiko.

BIBLIOGRAPHICAL REFERENCES

Antoni, Klaus J. *Der weisse Hase von Inaba: Vom Mythos zum Märchen*. Wiesbaden: Franz Steiner, 1982.

Gardiner, Alan H. *The Library of Chester Beatty: Description of a Hieratic Papyrus with a Mythological Story, Love-Songs and Other Miscellaneous Texts*. London, 1931.

Hubaux, Jean. "La déesse et le passeur d'eau." In *Mélanges offerts à M. Octave Navarre par ses élèves et ses amis*. Toulouse: Édouard Privat, 1935.

Janson, Horst Woldemar. *Apes and Ape Lore in the Middle Ages and the Renaissance*. London, 1935.

Lefebvre, Gustave. *Romans et contes égyptiens de l'époque pharaonique*. Paris: Adrien Maisonneuve, 1949.

Lévy, Isidore. "Autour d'un roman mythologique égyptien." *Annuaire de l'Institut de philologie et d'histoire orientales et slaves* 4 (1936).

8

An Unknown Tokyo

I HAD NOT visited Japan before the first editions of this book came out there. But between 1977 and 1988, I was able to go there five times, thanks to several institutions, to which I again express my gratitude: the Japan Foundation, the Suntory Foundation, the Japan Productivity Center, the Ishizaka Foundation, and finally, the International Research Center for Japanese Studies (Nichibunken).

The Japan Foundation was intent on presenting diverse aspects of the country to me over a period of six weeks. After letting me see Tokyo, Osaka, Kyoto, Nara, and Isa, the foundation had my distinguished colleagues Professors Yoshida Teigo and Fukui Katsuyoshi take me to the Noto Peninsula and the Oki Islands in the Sea of Japan. I am indebted to the Suntory Foundation for the opportunity to acquaint myself with the Inland Sea and Shikoku. In 1983 Professor Yoshida Teigo was kind enough to invite me to accompany him to the Iheya, Izena, and Kudaka Islands of the Ryukyu Archipelago, and to participate modestly in his ethnographic investigations. Three years later, during another stay, I wanted to visit Kyushu. That journey, lasting more than a week, would not have been possible without the company of Mrs. Watanabe Yasu, who was a peerless guide and interpreter beginning with my first stay.

I have innumerable debts of gratitude toward Professor Kawada Junzo, first and foremost for his translation of this book. In 1986, moreover, he revealed to me a Tokyo unknown to most foreign visitors, taking me up the Sumidagawa in a traditional boat, and following the twists and turns of the canals that crisscross the city to the east and west of the river.

At the time of my first visits, my Paris laboratory had a program in place for the study of the notion of work as conceived by various societies at different times and in different environments. I therefore expressed the wish for my trips to be organized as a function of that type of problem, to allow me to be in contact with city or village artisans, even in remote corners of the country. Although I have enduring memories of the museums, the temples of

Nara, and the sanctuaries of Ise, most of my time was devoted to meetings with weavers, dyers, kimono painters (professions that also interested my wife, a specialist in the textile arts), and also potters, forgers, wood turners, gold beaters, lacquer decorators, carpenters, fishermen, sake brewers, cooks, and pastry chefs, along with puppeteers and traditional musicians.

I gleaned precious information from them on how the Japanese understand work: not as the action of human beings on inert matter, in the Western manner, but as an establishment of an intimate relationship between humans and nature. On another level, certain Noh plays, which give pride of place to humble domestic tasks, confirm that notion by conferring a poetic value on them (thus making the Greek *poiēsis* coincide with the artistic sense of "poetry").

The relationship between the human individual and nature, which I had somewhat idealized in thinking about Japan before I went there, held other surprises in store. Traveling in the country, I perceived that the cult of natural beauties, illustrated—to Western eyes—by your marvelous gardens, the love of blossoming cherry trees, floral art, and even your cuisine, could accommodate an extreme brutality toward the natural environment. The journey up the river was a shock for me, since I was still picturing the Sumida in terms of Hokusai's exquisite albums, *Ehon Sumidagawa ryōgan ichiran*. It is true that a foreign visitor who knows Paris through ancient engravings would have the same reaction to the banks of the Seine as they exist today, though the contrast is no doubt less great, and the transition between the past and the present less abrupt. (Nonetheless, despite what I was told, modern Tokyo did not strike me as ugly. The irregular layout of the buildings gives an impression of diversity and freedom, unlike Western cities, where the monotonous alignment of the houses along streets and avenues compels the passerby to walk between two walls.)

In fact, it is probably that absence of a clear-cut distinction between humankind and nature that also explains the right the Japanese bestow on themselves (by one of those perverse chains of reasoning to which they sometimes resort, in the case of whaling, for example) to give priority sometimes to one, sometimes to the other, and to sacrifice nature if necessary to the needs of human beings. Are the two not interdependent?

I saw that as a particular explanation for the

"double standard," which, my Japanese colleagues taught me, provided a key to understanding their history. In a sense, it can even be said that Japan has found an original solution to the major problem of our time, the fact that, within a century, the global population has grown from fewer than two billion people to six billion. For Japan has established on its territory coastal regions so densely populated that they form an uninterrupted succession of cities coexisting alongside a nearly uninhabited mountainous interior. That coexistence also marks an opposition between two mental worlds, that of science, industry, and commerce, and one that continues to lend itself to beliefs coming from the fount of ages.

That "double standard" also has a temporal dimension. Phenomenally rapid development took Japan within a few decades a distance that the West had taken centuries to travel. As a result, Japan was able to modernize even while maintaining a close connection to its spiritual roots.

I devoted most of my professional life to studying mythology and to showing the extent to which that mode of thought remains legitimate. Therefore, I could only be profoundly attuned to the vitality that myths retain in Japan. I never felt so close to a remote past as on the little islands of the Ryukyu, among the coppices, rocks, caves, natural wells, and springs considered so many manifestations of the sacred. In Kudakashima, someone pointed out to us the place where the divine visitors appeared, bearers of the five kinds of seeds with which the primordial fields were planted. For residents, these events did not unfold in a mythic time. They happened yesterday, they are happening today, they will even happen tomorrow, since the gods who set foot there return every year and, over the entire expanse of the island, sacred rites and places give proof of their real presence.

Perhaps because their written history began at a relatively recent date, the Japanese quite naturally located its roots in myths. I became convinced of that in Kyushu, which according to the texts was the theater of their most ancient mythology. At this stage, questions of historicity do not arise: without anyone feeling troubled by it, two sites can compete for the honor of having welcomed the god Ninigi-no-mikoto upon his descent from heaven. And the majesty of the place where the sanctuary of Ōhirume (the goddess Amaterasu) stands leads people to embrace the old narrative of her retreat to the cave, too sacred for anyone to approach, but which can be glimpsed from afar. One has only to count the number of buses disgorging visitors who have come on pilgrimage to be persuaded that the great founding myths, the grandiose landscapes where tradition places them, maintain a real-life continuity between legendary times and contemporary sensibilities.

It has been almost half a century since, in writing *Tristes Tropiques*, I expressed my anxiety about two perils threatening humanity: that it would forget its own roots, and that it would be crushed under its own numbers. Japan, perhaps alone among nations, has until now been able to find a balance between fidelity to the past and the transformations brought about by science and technology. No doubt it is primarily beholden in this respect to the fact that it was ushered into modern times by a restoration and—unlike France, for example—not by a revolution. Its traditional values were thus protected from collapse. But it is beholden as well to a population that long remained at the ready, sheltered from a critical and systematic turn of mind whose contradictory excesses have undermined Western civilization. Even today, the foreign visitor admires the eagerness that everyone in Japan displays to perform his duty, the cheerful goodwill that, compared to the social and moral climate of his home country, seem to the traveler key virtues of the Japanese people. May they long maintain that precious balance between the traditions of the past and the innovations of the present, and not only for their own good, since humanity as a whole finds in them an example worth contemplating.

9

Interview with Junzo Kawada

In 1993 Claude Lévi-Strauss granted an interview to Junzo Kawada for Japan National Television (NHK). The first part, dealing primarily with Americanist anthropology, was followed by remarks on Japan. What follows is the transcription of that second part, whose wandering, conversational tone has been retained; the repetitions and marks of orality characteristic of such exchanges have not been omitted.

C. Lévi-Strauss: My father, like all artists of his generation, loved Japanese prints. And he gave them to me as gifts. I received the first one at the age of six and was immediately, absolutely fascinated. Throughout my childhood, the high marks I received at school were rewarded with the gift of a print, which my father pulled out of his cardboard boxes.

J. KAWADA: What are your favorites? The *ukiyo-e* painters?

C. LÉVI-STRAUSS: I particularly admire the painters of the archaic period—well, those of the Kambun period, or even a little later: Kaigetsudō, Moronobu, and a few others. But in the end, those are things you see in museums, and nowhere else! I became very interested in Kuniyoshi's art, often considered decadent—that's what they call him—but I find there's a phenomenal inventiveness there and a violence that finds expression in his art. What appealed to me for a long while were his early prints, done in about 1830, illustrating the translation of *Suikoden*; well, Bakin did a translation from the Chinese at that time. Not only do I find them very beautiful, but they also seem interesting to me from an ethnological standpoint, because they show quite well the view the nineteenth-century Japanese had of a very ancient China.

But those are altogether different things: that's really popular art, we're dealing with the *namazu-e*, that is, with the 1855 earthquake during the Ansei period, which revived an ancient mythology that certain Japanese milieus may find a little shocking today. Because, for example, you see a rich man who is obliged to excrete his wealth, and the earthquake—well, the *yonaoshi*, "renewal of the world"—allows the down-and-out, the poor, to appropriate the wealth of the rich.

What's rather curious, you know, is that the symbolism, which might appear altogether local, bizarre, also existed in our Middle Ages. In the twelfth century, for example, when a new pope was elected (which in a sense was a *yonaoshi*, a renewal of the world), the pope-elect had to sit at the front of the basilica on a chair with holes in it—called the "stercorary chair," that is, the excremental chair. From there he distributed riches, as a biblical psalm was recited: "He raiseth up the poor . . . that he may set him with princes" [113:7–8]. That is exactly the same symbolism we see in the *namazu-e*. So that invites us to reflect on what is fundamental in the human spirit, which can be found in extremely different contexts.

The *namazu* is the cause of the earthquakes in Japan; in America, or at least in certain corners of America, the cause is a fish that belongs to the Scorpaenides family. And that family is represented in Japan by the *okoze* fish, which is an offering to the god of the mountains. Obviously, mountains and earthquakes are linked in a certain sense, so that what is proper to the *namazu* in Japan is proper to the *okoze* in the Americas.

And then, also in the Americas, catfish, well, *namazu*, are the cause of illnesses. Now the word *namazu*, if I am not confusing it with the same character, designates both the fish and a skin disease, a disease the fish is supposed both to cause and to cure. So there is in that an entire realm, fairly obscure in the Americas, much more obscure than in Japan, which would merit being explored. For the Americanist, this is all very interesting.

J. KAWADA: Has your attachment to Japan been continuous—if not always conscious—since your childhood, or was it a new anthropological interest in Japan that developed later?

C. LÉVI-STRAUSS: I would not say that the interest was continuous. During my years in Brazil, I was entirely preoccupied with things from the Americas and no longer thought very much about Japan. But even in the United States during the [second world] war, I started to get interested in it again, very keenly so, while looking at objects in museums. And deep down, I didn't think I would ever go to Japan. That idea had not occurred to me. Then a wonderful invitation from the Japan Foundation arrived in 1977, almost like a bolt out of the blue. And I said to myself: now finally I'm going to see Japan, which I've thought about off and on my whole life!

J. KAWADA: Even before that invitation, you already had an interest in Japan . . .

C. LÉVI-STRAUSS: An anthropological interest, but perhaps not as extraordinary as it became after several stays in Japan.

J. KAWADA: The Nambikwara or Caduveo of Brazil and the Japanese are common descendants of the same distant ancestors. What is the continuity or discontinuity you have sensed between these two populations from different geographical and cultural regions?

C. LÉVI-STRAUSS: We all have the same ancestors, of course! And it is clear that, when you look at Japan, especially popular literature or mythology, you find echoes that remind the Americanist of things. It's just that you have to be careful, because it's not only between Japan and America; it's a three-handed game. What we find between Japan and America, or between America and Japan, we

also find in Insulindia, especially around the Celebes Islands. So there is a sort of triangular interplay, so to speak—in your writings, you like cultural triangulation. And we must not forget that
fifteen or twenty thousand years ago, Japan was
part of continental Asia, and similarly, Insulindia
was connected to continental Asia. So for millennia, there may have been population movements,
exchanges of ideas, and the construction of a sort
of common patrimony, bits of which we also find
in the Americas, Japan, and Insulindia.

J. KAWADA: What was your first impression of Japan
in 1977? Do you still find it pertinent today, in
1993, after so many experiences and studies in our
country?

C. LÉVI-STRAUSS: In an earlier conversation, you
asked me that question about Brazil. I told you:
when you land in the New World, the first thing,
the first impression, is nature. As for Japan, I will
tell you that the first impression, the strongest one,
is people. That is rather significant, because the
American continent was poor in human beings
but full of natural riches, while Japan, poor in natural resources, is by contrast very rich in human
beings. The sense of finding yourself confronted

with—I would not say a different humanity, that would be unlike me—but a humanity that was less worn down by revolutions and wars than in the old world, of finding a humanity that gives the sense that people are still at the ready, that they have the sense, however humble their social position may be, of performing a function that is necessary to society as a whole, and that they are perfectly at ease with that. I believe you have an eighteenth-century philosopher, Ishida Baigan, if I am not mistaken, who was the founder of the Shingaku movement and who insisted precisely on that moral aspect. For me, it is symbolized somewhat by the different ways we say "yes" in French and in Japanese. We say *oui*, you say *hai*. I have always had the impression—it may be altogether false, it may be a Loti impression, a backwards one—that there is much more in *hai* than in *oui*. That *oui* is a sort of passive acquiescence, whereas *hai* is a leap toward the interlocutor.

J. KAWADA: Indeed. On that subject, a little digression would be necessary. The interjection *hai* was a dialectal expression from Satsuma, the military province that, along with Chōshū, defeated the Tokugawa army and brought about the Meiji reformation. Those two provinces shared national power for half a century. During that time, at primary school and in the army, people were obliged to respond *hai* unanimously, as a sign of obedience, whereas in other regions, including Kyoto and Edo, the traditional word to respond affirmatively was *hee, hei, ee, nda,* or some other term. For our generation, which lived through the ultranationalist, militarist old regime in Japan before 1945, the word *hai* thus evokes the spirit of unconditional obedience to a higher power. All the same, that in no way changes what you said about Ishida Baigan's ideas.

C. LÉVI-STRAUSS: But let's come back to the beauty of Japanese nature. I would have a great deal to say about that because, as soon as you arrive in Japan—practically between Narita and Tokyo, because there are little bits of nature left and right—you discover a nature that is richer in the diversity of colors. And which seems better organized, perhaps, because in Europe vegetation is for the most part irregular—did not Baudelaire define it that way: "le végétal irrégulier"?—and it is from those irregular elements that we try to create a regularity in our gardens. Whereas the elements of Japanese nature are much more regular: *sugi*, the Cryptomeria, rice fields, bamboo, tea plantations. All that introduces from the outset an element of regularities, with which you create, so to speak, a regularity on a higher order, a higher level: a regularity to the second degree.

J. KAWADA: In 1986, when you took a boat ride on the canals of Tokyo and to the island of Tsukuda, where we came on board, you told Mme Lévi-Strauss that you would like to live in that humble working-class neighborhood. What aspect of that neighborhood appealed to you?

C. LÉVI-STRAUSS: Tsukudajima was a shock. Because those little wooden houses, all surrounded by greenery, those fishermen wearing their work clothes, but who gave the impression somewhat of being dressed in the ancient manner, the small boat in which we navigated, all that reminded me from the start of Hokusai and the beautiful *Sumidagawa ryōgan ichiran*, "The Two Banks of the Sumida"; in other words, of something that was probably one of the greatest successes of civilization, on a par with Venice. In fact, what you revealed to me was a sort of Venice in Tokyo, of which I had no inkling. That was all profoundly touching for someone who, precisely, knew Japan only through ancient images. And so you're asking me if I found that anywhere else?

I would tell you that, when I went to Japan, many Japanese told me: "Above all, don't be daunted by Tokyo. Tokyo is an ugly city." Well, I did not have that impression at all in modern Tokyo, because I found myself liberated from something that I did not suspect was so constrictive in our civilizations, namely, streets! Streets with houses all stuck together, while the buildings in Tokyo are put up with much more freedom, so to speak, and constantly leave an impression of diversity.

Then, above all, when you get past those grand avenues with raised roadways—which are a real nightmare, there's no point kidding yourself—and make your way left and right into the side streets, you come upon little neighborhoods that, really, still evoke the city of another age. Ultimately, for the Parisian these neighborhoods represent an extraordinary luxury, because it is no longer possible in Paris to live in a small individual house surrounded by a little garden in the heart of the city. It is still, up to a certain point—probably not for long, I'm afraid—possible in Tokyo.

J. KAWADA: You always had a keen intellectual but also a gastronomical curiosity. Could you give us your comments on Japanese cuisine, based on your own experience?

C. LÉVI-STRAUSS: You know, I immediately liked Japanese food. Nevertheless, there were many new things for me. Of course, I was with the Indians of Brazil, I ate living larvae—raw, yes!—but I had never eaten raw fish; *sashimi* I was absolutely unfamiliar with.

J. KAWADA: Oh yes, raw carp!

C. LÉVI-STRAUSS: Yes, yes, and other fish as well. What I immediately liked about Japanese cuisine is also what had always appealed to me in *ukiyo-e*, and even in what is called "Yamato-e art" in general, namely, the care taken to leave colors in their pure state, to distinguish line and color: to apply a certain decomposition to the elements, so to speak, of which both our cuisine and our painting try to make a general synthesis.

But that way of leaving flavors in their pure state, in all their simplicity, of leaving the consumer with the task of organizing on his own the range of flavors he wishes to savor, that seems very appealing to me. I must say in fact that, since going to Japan, I no longer consume rice unless it is cooked in the Japanese manner. And thanks to your gifts, I was delighted to rediscover rice with *yakinori*, which, with that algae flavor, is as evocative of Japan for me as the madeleine was for Proust!

J. KAWADA: According to a myth that spread among foreign Japanophiles, the Japanese have the wisdom to live in harmony with nature. Nevertheless, in their concrete relations with nature in the wild, the Japanese do not have a well-developed practice. Rather, they set aside the wild parts, which represent about two-thirds of the area of Japan—these are called *yama*, which literally means "mountain," but with a connotation of "wild land."

The pollution and destruction of the environment are progressing at a furious pace in Japan, as you have seen, and at an even more accelerated rate, perhaps, since your last visit to Japan in 1988. How do you see the present situation of the relationship between man and nature in Japan, compared to the traditional idea of nature for the Japanese, conventionally conceived in idealized rather than real terms?

C. LÉVI-STRAUSS: You're altogether right. We formed a false idea on that score. In traveling just about everywhere, in the interior, in Shikoku, in Kyushu, along with so many marvelous impressions, I found the brutality with which Japan treats nature painful. But at the same time, you have to give Japan credit; you said it yourself, two-thirds of Japan is uninhabited nature. There are not many countries that were able to accomplish that feat of creating a phenomenal urban civilization that is at the same time respectful of a large part of its territory.

But the Western illusion comes, I believe, from the fact that the Japanese showed the West that it was possible to use nature as a raw material, to create an art based entirely on natural elements. That is what you do with *ikebana*, and that is also what you do with Japanese gardens. I would readily say that ordinary Japanese nature, the one people see, already represents a garden of sorts, when compared to our own. And that your gardens represent gardens to the second power. I had a very profound sense of that in Kyushu, while visiting that village of Chiran.

J. KAWADA: Of Chiran, yes . . .

C. LÉVI-STRAUSS: It is still practically intact. You find dwellings there that belonged to ancient Samurai from the *daimyō* of the place, and each one with a very beautiful house and a small garden. But a small garden of a luxury and refinement that, as you went from one house to another, were of a great diversity; as if each owner, with his own personality, had wanted to create from natural elements an original work that stands apart from that of his neighbor, as much as the work of a great painter can be distinguished from that of another.

That's what has been taken in the West to be a love of nature. So the reality is more complicated!

J. KAWADA: Through your anthropological research, you have revalorized the wild, the *sauvage*. Could you tell us very briefly, could you tell the Japanese—and given the current state of Japanese culture—why it is important to preserve the *sauvage*?

C. LÉVI-STRAUSS: I did not so much valorize the *sauvage*, I just wanted to show that the *sauvage* persists in all of us. And since it is still present in us, we would be wrong to have contempt for it when it is outside us.

That is true, I believe, of all civilizations. But what I greatly admired as an anthropologist is the

capacity of Japan, in its most modern manifestations, to feel in solidarity with its most remote past.
For our part, we are well aware that we have
"roots," but we have the greatest difficulty recon-
necting with them. There is a gulf we no longer
manage to bridge. We look at them from the other
side of the gulf. In Japan, there is a type of continuity, so to speak, or of solidarity, which may not
be eternal but that still exists today.

J. KAWADA: As you've written, Japan constitutes in
many areas "a backwards world" when compared
to France. In artisanry, which interests you in particular, it can be seen in a fairly typical fashion.
But to shed light on the cause of these differences
in customs, one would no doubt have to take into
account ecological and physical factors as well as
cultural ones.

C. LÉVI-STRAUSS: We would have to qualify that a
bit, because that "backwards" Japan was first noticed not by the French but by Portuguese and
Italian missionaries in the sixteenth century. After
that, in the late nineteenth century, Basil Chamberlain, who wrote on the subject, was English. So
it's not about France and Japan in particular but
rather about the Old World and Japan, since even

China in that respect does not display these inversions.

I believe you are completely right to say that one must take into account ecological, historical factors. But I wonder whether that's enough. Because although certain explanations on the technical and economic order can be found for the fact that the crosscut saw is pulled rather than pushed, it would be necessary to seek another explanation for why the needle is pushed onto the thread and not the thread into the eye of the needle, why the cloth is pricked on the needle and not the needle stuck into the cloth, why the potter's wheel is pushed with one foot in the Old World but in Japan with the other foot, and why it turns clockwise in one case but counterclockwise in the other, why, in ancient Japan, people mounted horses from the right, whereas we mount them from the left, why the horse was put in the stable backwards instead of head first, and so on.

J. KAWADA: To study these "topsy-turvy" phenomena in France and Japan, I think it's also necessary to take into account historical vicissitudes, which we can follow through written or iconographic documents. What Luís Fróis noted in the sixteenth century, that in Japan people mounted horses from the right, can be explained by the habit that warriors had at the time of holding a long bow in their left hand, or "bow hand," *yunde*, and of seizing the reins with their right hand, or "horse hand," *mete*. Nevertheless, a few aspects of life, like certain bodily techniques, display an astonishing tenacity, despite the enormous changes that have come about in other aspects of life. For example, you said just now that "the potter's wheel is pushed with one foot in the Old World but in Japan with the other foot"; but in fact in Japan one does not push with the other foot, one pulls with the same foot, the right one. That provides another example confirming your hypothesis about the centripetal character of Japanese culture, which can be seen through the historical vicissitudes. What do you think of the relationship between these two realms—anthropological and historical—in general, and in particular in the case of the cultures of France and Japan?

C. Lévi-Strauss: These phenomena are altogether interesting, particularly for ethnologists. We find that even societies that have faith in history and advocate historical change, preserve, without even realizing it, many of these customs, which have not been threatened by the historical circumstances but remain, and which are in that way the traces of a very remote past. Nonetheless, in Europe, for example, you can try to draw a boundary line on the basis of whether people wash their hands in running water or in stagnant water. And I ask you the question—as a Japanese, when you wash your hands, do you stop up the basin or do you leave it open?

J. KAWADA: I tend to leave it open.

C. LÉVI-STRAUSS: So do I. I leave it open because that's probably an atavism of eastern Europe, where my ancestors come from.

J. KAWADA: Really!

C. LÉVI-STRAUSS: Really. Whereas in the Latin world, there will be a tendency to stop up the basin. I noted a very nice example of that kind, in fact, in the book I'm publishing in a few weeks,* and which deals with a question of art. In it I'm concerned with an eighteenth-century philosopher, a Jesuit priest who was interested in colors:

---

* Claude Lévi-Strauss, *Regarder écouter lire* (Paris: Plon, 1993), pp. 127–136.

Father Castel. He says somewhere: "The French don't like yellow. They find it drab, they leave it to the English." Then, last year, when Queen Elizabeth II came to France on an official visit, the French fashion newspapers made fun of her a little because one day she wore a yellow suit, and the French said: that yellow, it's bizarre, it's unseemly. So there are invariants that can last an extremely long time through the vicissitudes of history, and I think that is the very subject of the ethnologist's work.

J. KAWADA: How do you see the contrast in cultural orientation between France and Japan, especially the French orientation toward the universal and the Japanese orientation toward an elaboration of the particular?

Paul Valéry wrote that it is the particularity of the French to feel like universal human beings and to specialize in the universal. The Japanese, conversely, have never dreamed of being universal humans. Rather, they had a tendency to feel special, very different from others, believing themselves inscrutable to strangers, even while elaborating their artistic and technical particularities. At least up to now, the Japanese have been receivers more than transmitters in international cultural exchanges.

C. LÉVI-STRAUSS: You're asking at least two questions.

For the first, one could say that Western logic is founded in part on the structure of language. In that respect, it seems very significant to me that the structure of the Japanese language did not determine the structure of a particular logic but rather the structure of a body language—which we were talking about a moment ago. That is, one language turned toward abstraction and theory, while the other—but with the same concern for analysis, for precision in the details, for the decomposition of reality into its essential parts—turned toward practical action.

For your second question, you say that Japan was more receptive than creative.

Obviously, it was subject to many influences, especially Chinese and Korean influences, before falling under the influence of Europe and North America. It's just that what seems striking to me in the case of Japan is that it assimilated them so thoroughly that it made them into something different. And all the same, I don't want to forget another aspect, which is that, before falling under any of those influences, you had a civilization, that of the Jmon period, which created not only the most ancient ceramic that exists for humankind but a ceramic of an inspiration so original that we find no equivalent to it anywhere else in the world. It cannot be compared to anything else. So then, I would say there is proof of a Japanese specificity that was there originally, and that Japanese specificity was always able to elaborate elements received from elsewhere to make them into something original.

You know, for a long time we were considered in Japan a kind of model that had to be followed. I have often heard young Japanese say—in the face of the tragic events that bankrupted the West and the crises that are currently tearing it apart: "There are no longer any models; we no longer have a model to follow, and it is really up to us to create our own model." All I can wish for and ask of Japan is that the Japanese will be able to keep for that model (which, in fact, has received so much from the rest of the world) the same originality they had in the past. Through that originality, they can enrich us.

J. KAWADA: Do you believe there might be an optimal stage of human life in the history of humankind? If so, do you situate it in the past or in the future?

C. LÉVI-STRAUSS: Certainly not in the future, I rule that out! First, that's not the anthropologist's job — our job is the past. That question is extremely difficult to answer. Because it would not be enough to say: I would have liked to live in this or that age. I would have to know what social position I would have occupied at that time! Because, obviously, I might have . . . We always think of those ages in the past from the standpoint of the most favored class, and certainly not from the others!

So I will not name any era in particular. I would say: an era where there was still, between human beings and nature, between humans and natural species, a certain balance; where human beings could not claim to be the masters and lords of creation but knew they were an integral part of that creation, along with other living beings, which humans had to respect. During what era was that the best, the most true? It has been variously true in various ages. The only thing I can say is: certainly not in the present!

J. KAWADA: And not in the future either?

C. LÉVI-STRAUSS: And in the future, I fear, less and less.

Sources

1. "The Place of Japanese Culture in the World"

The text of this lecture, delivered in Kyoto on March 9, 1988, during the opening session of the International Research Center for Japanese Studies (Nichibunken), was published for the first time in Japanese in the May 1988 issue of the Tokyo review *Chūo kōron*. It then appeared in *Revue d'esthétique* 18 (1990): 9–21.

2. "The Hidden Face of the Moon"

Closing session (Saturday, October 13) of the colloquium entitled "Japanese Studies in France," Paris, October 8–13, 1979, pp. 255–263.

3. "The White Hare of Inaba"

Note on the American versions of the story of the white hare of Inaba, published in Chiwaki Shinoda, ed., *Mythes, symboles et littérature 2.* Nagoya: Rakur-shoin, 2002, pp. 1–6.

4. "HERODOTUS IN THE CHINA SEA"

In *Poikilia: Études offertes à Jean-Pierre Vernant.* Paris: Éditions de l'École des Hautes Études en Sciences Sociales, 1987, pp. 25–32.

5. "SENGAI: THE ART OF ACCOMMODATING ONESELF TO THE WORLD"

Introduction to *Sengaï moine zen 1750–1837: Traces d'encre.* Paris: Musées, 1994, pp. 19–30.

6. "DOMESTICATING STRANGENESS"

Preface to R. P. Luís Fróis, *Européens et Japonais: Traité sur les contradictions et différences de moeurs (1585).* Paris: Chandeigne, 2009 (1998), pp. 7–11.

7. "THE SHAMELESS DANCE OF AME NO UZUME"

Excerpted from "Quelques réflexions autour du dieu god Saruta-Hito." In the *Annual Report of the Saruta-hiko Forum* (Ise, Japan) 4 (2001): 10–16.

8. "AN UNKNOWN TOKYO"

Preface to the most recent Japanese edition of *Tristes Tropiques* (2001), pp. 268–269.

9. "INTERVIEW WITH JUNZO KAWADA"

Interview conducted in Paris for Japan National Television (NKH), 1993.

About the Author

CLAUDE LÉVI-STRAUSS was born on November 28, 1908, in Brussels. He held the chair of social anthropology at the Collège de France from 1959 to 1982 and was elected a member of the Académie Française in 1973. He died in Paris on October 30, 2009.

AMONG HIS WORKS:

La vie familiale et sociale des Indiens Nambikwara. Paris: Société des Américanistes, 1948. [*Family and Social Life of the Nambikwara Indians.* Translated by Eileen Sittler. New Haven, Conn.: Human Relations Area Files, 197?]

Les structures élémentaires de la parenté. Paris: PUF, 1949; The Hague: Mouton, 1967. [*The Elementary Structures of Kinship.* Translated by James Harle Bell, John Richard von Sturmer, and Rodney Needham. Boston: Beacon, 1969.]

Race et histoire. Paris: UNESCO, 1952. [*Race and History.* Paris: UNESCO, 1952.]

Tristes tropiques. Paris: Plon, 1955. [*Tristes Tropiques.* Translated by John Russell. New York: Atheneum, 1961.]

Anthropologie structurale. 2 vols. Paris: Plon, 1958. [*Structural Anthropology.* Translated by Claire Jacobson and Brooke Grundefest Schoepf. New York: Basic, 1963.]

Le totémisme aujourd'hui. Paris: PUF, 1962. [*Totemism.* Translated by Rodney Needham. Boston: Beacon, 1963.]

La pensée sauvage. Paris: Plon, 1962. [*The Savage Mind.* Chicago: University of Chicago Press, 1966.]

Mythologiques. Paris: Plon, 1964–1971. Vol. 1, *Le cru et le cuit.* Vol. 2, *Du miel aux cendres.* Vol. 3, *L'origine des manières de table.* Vol. 4, *L'homme nu.* [*Introduction to the Study of Mythology.* Translated by John Weightman and Doreen Weightman. New York: Harper & Row, 1969–1981. Vol. 1, *The Raw and the Cooked.* Vol. 2, *From Honey to Ashes.* Vol. 3, *The Origin of Table Manners.* Vol. 4, *The Naked Man.*]

Anthropologie structurale II. Paris: Plon, 1973. [*Structural Anthropology II.* Translated by Monique Layton. Harmondsworth, U.K.: Penguin, 1973.]

La voie des masques. 2 vols. Geneva: Albert Skira, 1975; revised, augmented edition followed by *Trois excursions.* Paris: Plon, 1979. [*The Way of the Masks.* Translated by Sylvia Modelsky. Seattle: University of Washington Press, 1982.]

Le regard éloigné. Paris: Plon, 1983. [*The View from Afar.* Translated by Joachim Neugroschel and Phoebe Hoss. New York: Basic, 1985.]

Paroles données. Paris: Plon, 1984. [*Anthropology and Myth: Lectures, 1951–1982.* Translated by Roy Willis. New York: Blackwell, 1987.]

La potière jalouse. Paris: Plon, 1985. [*The Jealous Potter.* Translated by Bénédicte Chorier. Chicago: University of Chicago Press, 1988.]

Histoire des lynx. Paris: Plon, 1991. [*The Story of Lynx.* Translated by Catherine Tihanyi. Chicago: University of Chicago Press, 1995.]

Regarder écouter lire. Paris: Plon, 1993. [*Look, Listen, Read.* Translated by Brian C. J. Singer. New York: Basic, 1997.]

Oeuvres. Paris: Gallimard, 2008.